CUTHBERT GARRAWAY

INTRODUCTION TO BEEKEEPING

Your Beginner's Handbook to the
World of Beekeeping
(2024 Crash Course)

Contents

1

The logical consider of nectar bees

It was not until the 18th century that the precise think about of bee colonies was conducted by European normal logicians and begun to get it the intriguing and mystery world of bee science. Swammerdam, René Antoine Ferchault de Réaumur, Charles Cap, and François Huber were compelling among these investigate pioneers. Swammerdam and Réaumur were moreover the primary to utilize a magnifying lens and dismemberment to get it the nectar bees' inside biology. Réaumur was among the primary to form a walled glass perception hive to assist screen hives behavior. He found rulers laying eggs in open cells but however had small thought how to fertilize a ruler; no one had ever seen a ruler and ramble mating, and a few theories recommended that rulers were "self-fertile," whereas others claimed that a fog or "miasma" exuding from the rambles fertilized rulers without any physical interaction. By perception and testing, Huber was the to begin with to appear that Rulers are physically inseminated by rambles past the boundaries of hives, as a rule a extraordinary remove separated.

Utilizing the fashion of Réaumur, Huber set up upgraded glass-walled perception hives and sectional hives, which may well be opened like a book's clears out. This permitted assessment of person wax combs and enormously moved forward coordinate hive action observation. Huber contracted an collaborator, François Burns, to form standard reports, perform fastidious ponders, and take nitty gritty records for more than twenty a long time, whereas he went dazzle some time recently he was twenty. Huber affirmed that a hive is composed of one ruler, who is the mother of both the colony's female laborers and male rambles. He was too the primary to report that mating with rambles happens exterior of hives and that rulers are inseminated by a arrangement of continuous male ramble matches, tall within the discuss at a significant separate from their hive.

In 1768/1770, for illustration, Thomas Wildman detailed middle of the road stages within the move from the ancient beekeeping to the cutting edge, clarifying changes over the destroying old beekeeping based on criticism so that the bees were not to be annihilated to extricate the nectar. For case, Wildman introduced a parallel combine of wooden bars over the beat of a straw hive or cynic (with a isolated straw beat to be afterward mounted) "so that there are in add up to seven bars" [in a 10-inch (250 mm) hive] "in which the bees settle their combs." He too clarified the utilize of these hives in a multi-story structure, portending the current utilize of supers: he clarified the presentation (at the proper time) of progressive straw hives underneath and at last dispensing with those over when free of brood and filled with nectar so that the bees may be kept independently at the collect for the ensuing season.

development of the hive plans

Langstroth's concept for free comb hives was discovered by apiarists and inventors on both sides of the Atlantic, and a variety of mobile comb hives were created in England, France, Germany, and the United States. In every nation, a classic design emerged: in the US, Dadant and Langstroth hives are still widely used; in France, the De-Layens trough-hive gained popularity; in the UK, a British National hive became common as late as the 1930s; and in Scotland, the smaller Smith hive is still widely used. Until the late 20th century, the traditional trough hive was used in several Nordic nations, Russia, and other places. In certain places, it is still used today. As for national hive designs, Sweden, Denmark, Germany, France, and Italy all have their own, although the Langstroth and Dadant designs are still widely used in the US and other parts of Europe. The habitat, floral quality, and reproductive traits of the many native honey bee subspecies in each bioregion led to the development of regional hive variations.

Due to their common characteristics—all of which are square or rectangular, have compact wooden frames, and are made up of a base, brood cabinet, honey super, crown board, and roof—there are very few variances in the sizes of these hives. In the past, cedar, oak, or cypress wood was used to build hives; but, in recent years, injection-molded, dense polystyrene colonies have grown in popularity.

In order to stop the queen from laying eggs in cells next to those that contain honey intended for human consumption between the brood-box and honey supers, hives frequently use queen excluders. Since mite pests were introduced in the 20th century, hive floors are typically covered for part of the year, if not all of it, with a wire mesh and flexible tray.

Developed in Australia in 2015 by Cedar Anderson and his father Stuart Anderson, the Flow Hive technology eliminates the need for expensive centrifuge devices while extracting honey.

2

Advantages of Beekeeping

The need of beekeeping is becoming more and more apparent to people worldwide. Perhaps you're wondering what beekeeping can do for you, and what improvements it can bring about. Beekeeping is undoubtedly a useful profession. There is never a waste of time spent on beekeeping. You will feel proud of yourself if you understand the bees and can effectively maintain the colony. There is pressure on bees worldwide as well. Its population is declining as a result of a variety of reasons working together, such as the widespread use of pesticides in agriculture and global warming, both of which have the unintended effect of killing a significant number of bees.

The primary advantages of being a beekeeper are as follows: practical and worthwhile You'll start creating significant and beneficial things for the planet. You can make your own honey by beekeeping. It is a well-liked product that you can earn from. There will be a ton of honey available for you to utilize. Because of the enormous need for newborns worldwide, supply seldom ever keeps up with demand. Nevertheless, it's important to remember that not all beekeepers produce honey and do so for financial gain.

Gather more hive products.

You will start producing other goods we have seen from beekeeping in addition to honey. These beehive products are not inexpensive on the market. As the primary by-product of your beekeeping enterprise, you should try to gather one of these substitute beehive goods in large quantities. In addition to the honey they collect and sell, beekeepers who operate on a large enough scale do profit handsomely from other beehive products. Later on, we'll talk about these.

Participate in safeguarding

You can help with the beekeeping community by learning to keep bees. It is possible to let conventional bee colonies regenerate wild bee colonies through beekeeping. The genetic variety of the entire species and the many benefits of functional genetic diversity are also preserved by the wild population of bees.

How apiculturists work

With time, beekeeping has increased. There are certain distinct ways in which beekeeping has changed from its early days compared to today. The primary tool used in beekeeping nowadays is the hive. There are a lot of colonies that look like tree hollows, or the beekeepers utilized log hives in the past.

In the past, beekeeping was done by farmers who owned huge areas of land, frequently for an extended period of time, or by placing beehives in the woods. The reason behind it has been ascribed to the necessity of discouraging bees from interacting with people and other animals. From their hive, bees can occasionally become extremely aggressive and bite any animal or human that comes within a particular radius of the hive. Over time, improvements in understanding the honey bee and its characteristics have made it feasible to keep honey bees close to home.

Honey bee colonies that are unable to go on stinging sprees without any provocation have been produced by beekeepers with the aid of selective breeding and other beekeeping management techniques. These developments simplified the process of maintaining bees in remote areas. Urban beekeeping is now possible thanks to advancements in our understanding of honeybee violence. Many citizens can keep bees in urban areas if the proper safety measures are implemented and protection is the top priority for the beekeeper.

The innovations in beehives today The primary tool used in beekeeping was the beehive. These beehives have come a long way and experienced a significant transition into what they are now throughout time. Techniques that facilitate the production of specific beehive products over others are frequently used in modern hives. This unquestionable advancement in beekeeping technology enables honey bee colonies to survive long after beehive products are processed.

Since extracting honey would destroy much of the brood comb, which is typically found close to the beehive's entrance, previous beehives—including the log hive—made the honey bee colony's perpetual life impossible.

The main swarms used in beekeeping nowadays are the Warré, Top Bar, Langstroth, and conventional British hives. The other two, though less prevalent, are the Dadant and Layens hives, which are still used appropriately. The appropriateness of these hives varies depending on the preferences of individual beekeepers as well as the colony's orientation—vertical or horizontal.

Important aspects of beekeeping to take into consideration The main things you will need to think about before you start beekeeping are listed below.

1. The Area Around the Beehive You'll need to consider where to place the bees once you've decided to house them. Apiaries, also referred to as bee yards, are places where bees are kept. The regulations governing beekeeping differ from state to state and country to country, so you'll need to check with the local authorities.

In order to avoid future arguments, you should discuss your plans with neighbors and relatives if you plan to raise bees in your garden.

The ideal kind of hive to keep your bees in will need to be chosen as your next task.

2. Beehive Styles: • Langstroth Beehive • A Top Bar Beehive It was created more than 15 years ago and is named after its previous creator, Rev. L.L. Langstroth. This type of beehive is popular in North America and New Zealand and is generally preferred by both commercial and hobbyist beekeepers. Simple cleaning, a small size with plenty of room between the brood chambers and supers, easily removable frames for easy bee division and examination, and the ability to reuse beehives are just a few of its advantages. The primary drawback of this type of hive is that it disturbs the bees more than other hive types when being inspected.

Top-bar Beehive The topbar beehive is typically utilized because it is easy to install and long-lasting. With a top-bar hive, bees are less likely to become sidetracked during inspections, resulting in higher-quality honey production. But in comparison to the other two hive layouts discussed above, the top-bar hive helps bees produce more wax and less honey. Since the combs are transparent, they are exposed to all ambient conditions, which can frequently be too harsh for the bees, and they typically need to build new combs for each inspection.

The Warré hive is an excellent option for individuals who are too busy to regularly interact with the bees because it is much simpler to manage than other colonies.

British-Style National Beehive Usually rather common throughout the United Kingdom. Its price, simplicity of assembly, and great success are among its advantages. Its brood box is significantly smaller than typical, according to the majority of beekeepers who have used it. The issue can be resolved by using a different brood box to operate it.

3. A sunny, partially shaded area with a nearby water source, such as a pond, is usually the safest site to install the beehive. It is recommended that the hive be oriented towards the south and have a windbreak fence to the north. The bees can find it convenient to collect nectar and return to their hives fast, thus a position next to a flower field is much more ideal.

Finding out about any possible predators of bees and determining whether or not they would enter the hive quickly are also wise decisions. You wouldn't want to put your bee colony at risk of predators after investing a lot of your valuable time and resources in the laborious task.

4. Other Essential Items You'll Need Although honey is usually the main source for beekeeping, as previously said, people wish to work in the beekeeping industry for a variety of reasons. Bees must be treated very carefully since, as you may know, they can sting humans painfully and go crazy at the least provocation. Thus, when a beekeeper walks outside to tend to the hives or harvest honey on a daily basis, he could need some protection. Anybody who keeps bees must purchase a beekeeper's mask, boots, jacket, hat, and scarf. This is the protective apparel that will help prevent stings from occurring during interactions with the bees. To gather honey, you'll need to purchase a honey extractor and a bee smoker. As you work on each hive object, the bee smoker helps to calm the bees and reduce their noise level. After gathering the combs rich in honey, the following step is to extract the honey and wax from the combs without damaging them. Here's when the Honey Extractor comes in useful. Without causing harm to the peanuts or wax, the honey extractor facilitates the extraction of honey from bee peanuts.

Honey extractors can be classified into two primary categories: automatic and manual. If you are new to beekeeping, you can begin with a simpler, more affordable fundamental manual honey extractor.

Impacts of stings and preventative steps

According to some beekeepers, getting stung a few times a season is crucial for the beekeeper's health, and the more stings a beekeeper receives, the less pain they cause. Phospholipase A2 (PLA), a sizable poisonous bee antigen, triggers a strong immune response in beekeepers, primarily IgG. Antibodies and bee sting frequency are correlated. Venom from bee stings can also be prevented and reduced by wearing protective gear that enables the wearer to pull off venom sacs and remove stings with a simple tug on the clothing. A worker bee is less likely to become stuck in clothing than in human skin, even if the stinger is barbed. In addition, precautions should be made to ensure that the stung region is not overly irritated if a beekeeper gets stung. After a bee stung, the first precaution to take is to remove the stinger without compressing the associated venom glands. Simple fingernail scraping is an effective and natural method. By doing this action, the injected venom can be prevented from spreading and the pain associated with the sting can subside more quickly. One safe method to prevent venom from spreading is to wash the affected area, even with soap and water. The stung region needs to be covered with ice or a cold compress as a last step.

Keeping Bees Safe

Safety is the most important factor in beekeeping. When near a beehive or apiary, people and animals are frequently at risk of receiving a honey bee sting. Having the right protection is also crucial for continuous, healthy beekeeping. Honeybees will get stung by the beekeeper, which could be harmful. It's possible for other people and animals to suffer losses, and the beekeeper could face legal action. Beekeeping therefore involves a great deal of upkeep of the apiary, beehive, and surrounding surroundings.

Utilizing the beekeeping room allows for healthy beekeeping in close proximity to other humans and animals. In a consistent 1:1 vertical climb ratio, honey bees exhibit vertical acceleration per horizontal distance. The placement of walls and screens around beehives allows honey bees to travel upward and away from people and animals in the area. To this goal, hedges are very beneficial. Additionally, the safest place to put hives is somewhere hidden from both human and animal traffic routes. It is possible to do urban beekeeping in highly developed town areas by placing the hives on rooftops.

Although they forage extremely well for food for their hives, bees rarely fly down to sting people from rooftops.

Insect costumes Starting with an apiculture outfit, beekeepers who work with or near bees are protected. Beekeepers used to be limited to wearing bulky clothing as their only line of defense. In contemporary beekeeping, the hive suit is preferred. Beekeepers could choose from a variety of outfit variations. Some are simple, like dresses and jackets for beekeeping, and others require airflow. The beekeeping cap, which protects the beekeeper's face and back, is another component of the mostly unmodified beekeeping attire.

Using smoke smoke to increase security is another beekeeping tool. They have a piece of equipment known as a bee smoker. Usually, bees are the ones to discharge it. The smoker produces smoke in part by burning fuel made of wood. Because of their innate aversion to smoke and difficulty stinging, honey bees are honey bee feeders. The beekeeper can complete the chores they set out to accomplish at the beehive while the bees are gathering pollen. Pheromones released when a bee stings or is squashed are trapped, creating a second smoke effect. Applying Sugar Water Some beekeepers are introducing the usage of sugar water as a health trend to reduce the likelihood of bee stings. Bees groom themselves and one another when sugar water is applied in a thin mist. As a result, the beekeeper does his business at the beehive.

Exercise caution when using machinery and equipment. The world of beekeeping employs a wide range of machinery. The quantity of tools you use depends on how big your beekeeping business is and how much you can afford to spend on specialist equipment. Numerous of these gadgets could be sharp, dry, or injure someone in various ways. Each machine used by the beekeeper has an operating handbook that they must read, and they must take safety procedures to guarantee the machine runs safely at all times.

Another area where emphasis should be placed on protection is with tools and other equipment used in beekeeping. When used improperly, these tools can hurt beekeepers. As a general rule, you should only use your tools for the tasks that have been given to you, and you should always use them with consideration for the safety of others around you.

Improvements in products and methods for beekeeping The cycle of beekeeping's evolution is continuous, albeit it frequently moves slowly at first. The latest developments in beekeeping have given beekeepers access to novel and incredibly exciting techniques. Beekeepers will also profit from growing beekeeping supplies, so don't fall behind. Among these noteworthy things are a number of pollination services. Beekeepers are gradually being hired by farmers to assist with the pollination tasks performed by honey bees. In addition to allowing their honey bees to pollinate plants in agricultural regions, beekeepers who offer these services relocate their colonies as needed.

Bee boxes In order to start new honey bee colonies, beekeepers split colonies and sell the splits as box bees. By embracing the ideas of package bee exchange, one beekeeper in a local community will provide a settlement for the next beekeeper.

Queen Bee Operations It is common for a honey bee hive to require the installation of a new queen bee. In many cases, it ensures the colony's continuing life and aids in colony genetic variety. It also calms the colony. Requeening is the technique utilized to do this.

Other Beehive Goods that may be Harvested Honey is the most visible byproduct of beekeeping. It is frequently utilized, mostly as a sweetener. On the other hand, some beekeeping products are harvested. While some of those objects have been around for a while, others have gained notoriety in recent years. Other goods made by honey bees besides honey are as follows: apiswax

The second most important beehive medication is beeswax, both in terms of quantity and popularity. Wax is used by bees to construct the foundations that house and nourish their young and store honey. These kinds of formations are called honeycombs. Groups of hexagons are formed by the wax. There are thousands of these cells on a rabbit's face. The comb often has two faces.

At high temperatures, beeswax freezes just below the water's boiling point.

Additionally flammable is the paper. Every day, maxing candles are used. It has historically been the demand of many Christian organizations that beeswax be used to make the candles used in religious ceremonies. Beeswax is utilized in cosmetic, pharmaceutical, and skin care goods such as soaps and lotions.

Another beehive item that is frequently used in contemporary beekeeping is pollen. It is utilized in many different contexts, but mostly as a health-promoting addition to milk. It has a lot of protein. Honey bees collect pollen from flowers through foraging, and the pollen is then processed into granules inside the beehive. In a honey bee colony, powder serves as the larvae's and queen bee's main source of nutrition. At times, a large number of bees will also eat any pollen.

Royal jelly The worker bees extract and feed the larvae a white fluid that resembles paste. Nurse bees in a colony of honey bees produce honey for five to fifteen days and feed the larvae with royal jelly for three days each. When choosing which larvae to raise to adulthood as queen bees, the honey bees feed them royal jelly throughout their whole life cycle.

Royal jelly can only be extracted in small quantities at a time by beekeepers using specialized instruments.

Royal jelly is commonly consumed by humans and, among other things, it helps to promote the formation of brain cells.

One important part of the propolis that honey bees collect is called propolis resins. Its antibacterial and purifying properties are why it is grown. When honey bees dislike a hole, gap, or fracture in their hive, propolis is utilized to seal it. It prevents bacteria formation in hives. The specific plant species and season that a colony's numerous foraging honey bees visit determine which propolis species are present.

3

Equipment Used in Beekeeping

Several colonies, the size of the operation, and the anticipated yield of honey all influence the equipment requirements. The exact tools required are a smoker, safety gear, hive apparatus parts, and tools for managing the honey harvest in addition to a hive.

The honey bee colony resides in an artificial structure called a hive. Over time, several different types of hives have been created. The Langstroth or traditional ten-frame hive is still used by the majority of beekeepers today. A set of boxes or hive bodies with suspended frames carrying a foundation or comb, an internal and exterior cover, a bottom board with an entry cleat or reducer, and a hive stand make up a typical colony. With the use of a queen excluder, the hive bodies housing the brood nest can be separated from the honey supers, which are used to store extra honey.

1. Hive stand: The hive stand is merely an optional piece of furniture that raises the bottom board (floor) of the hive off the ground. In turn, this treatment raises bottom board life, decreases hive humidity, and keeps grass and weeds out of the front door. One colony, two colonies, or a multi-colonial chain can all be supported by a single hive stand.

2. Bottom level: This level is used by bees for both takeoff and landing during foraging as well as serving as the floor of the colony. The settlement should be pushed slightly forward to stop rainfall from entering the hive because the bottom board is open at the top. Removable bottom boards with

a 7/8- or 3/8-inch front gap are sold by various bee supply dealers.

3. Bee bodies - The standard ten-frame hive body comes in four heights or depths (Figure 9). Most often, rearing larvae is done with the 9 5/8-inch-long full-depth hive body. With little interference, such huge units offer plenty of room for sizable, powerful brood fields. For honey supers, they're always excellent. When they're packed with sugar, though, they weigh more than sixty pounds and are hard to handle.

Super Dadant, also known as Illinois or super medium-depth, stands 6 5/8 inches tall. Standard-sized lumber cannot be cut well, even though this is the scale that works best for the honey supers. Certain beekeepers, especially those who construct their own boxes, choose for an intermediate level (7 5/8) that falls between the full- and medium-depth supers.

The easiest device to handle is the ultra shallow-depth model, which is 5 1/16 inches long and weighs approximately 35 pounds when filled with honey. The most money is spent building comb rooms per square inch on that model. It is generally not advised for novices to process section comb honey as it is a technical skill requiring close supervision.

Eight-plate hive bodies are a common practice among beekeepers. Originally imported, eight-frame hive boxes for the English garden are now available from a U.S. bee manufacturer. A set of three or five nucs, typically with normal deep frames, is typically used by beekeepers who are selling colonies of small starts (nucs) and raising queens. These are available from bee manufacturers and are constructed from cardboard (albeit the latter should only be used temporarily).

A number of management techniques are employed, contingent on the depth of the hive bodies in the hive brood field. One suggestion is to utilize a single full-depth hive body, which might provide the queen with all the room she needs to lay eggs. Thus, more room is needed for the brood nest to grow as much as possible and for storing food. Whether a kit is installed, a nucleus colony or division is first produced, or beekeepers decide to crowd bees for the production of comb honey, a single, full-depth brood chamber is typically utilized. Some beekeepers would rather utilize one shallow hive body for the brood field or two full-depth hive bodies. It is possible to swap combs between the two hive bodies by using hive bodies of the same shape. Beekeepers might choose to employ the brood nest, which has three shallow hive bodies, as an alternative to big fulldepth hive bodies. This method works well, but it requires more money and effort to assemble than the others because it requires thirty frames and three crates rather than only twenty.

4. The hive's main structural component is its frame and combs, which are hung beeswax combs. A sheet of beeswax or plastic foundation is used to construct the wooden or plastic beeswax comb in a man-made hive. The workers apply wax to wash out the base before using the pulled cells for brood rearing or storing honey and pollen.

A top bar, two end bars, and a bottom bar make up a through frame.

Bottom bars can be fractured, firm, or grooved; top bars can be grooved or wedged. While there can be benefits to some kinds over others, ultimately the choice comes down to personal taste and budget. The top bars of the hive body are supported on ledges or rabbets at their ends. For support on the recess, metal frames with spacers or V-shaped metal strips are also hammered. Regular commercial end bars feature shoulders to assist guarantee that there is enough room for bees to move between neighboring structures and box hands. The thin sheets of beeswax that make up the comb foundation are imprinted with patterns of worker-sized cells on both sides (Figure 10). Two popular forms of comb foundations can be distinguished by their relative thickness: A larger, more solid base can be employed in the brood chamber and frames for the processing experiment; otherwise, fragile surplus foundations are used to create segment comb honey, chunk honey, or cut-comb honey. Thicker foundations are typically used to support vertically exposed cables, thin fiber sheets, metal tops, or nylon strings. The initial cost, installation time, longevity, and anticipated period of use are all factors to take into account when choosing whether to invest in pure beeswax foundation in wooden or plastic frames or plastic beeswax foundation in plastic frames. Chemical buildings and foundations are becoming more and more prevalent.

Using the beeswax foundation in wooden frames requires that the interior of the frame be secured with either metal support pins or horizontal wires. Combs can be further improved by employing an embedded spur cable or by embedding parallel cables (28 or 30 gauges) with an electric current flowing through the base from a tiny transformer. Even a well-supported basis helps create well-drawn combs, but mastering this process takes time.

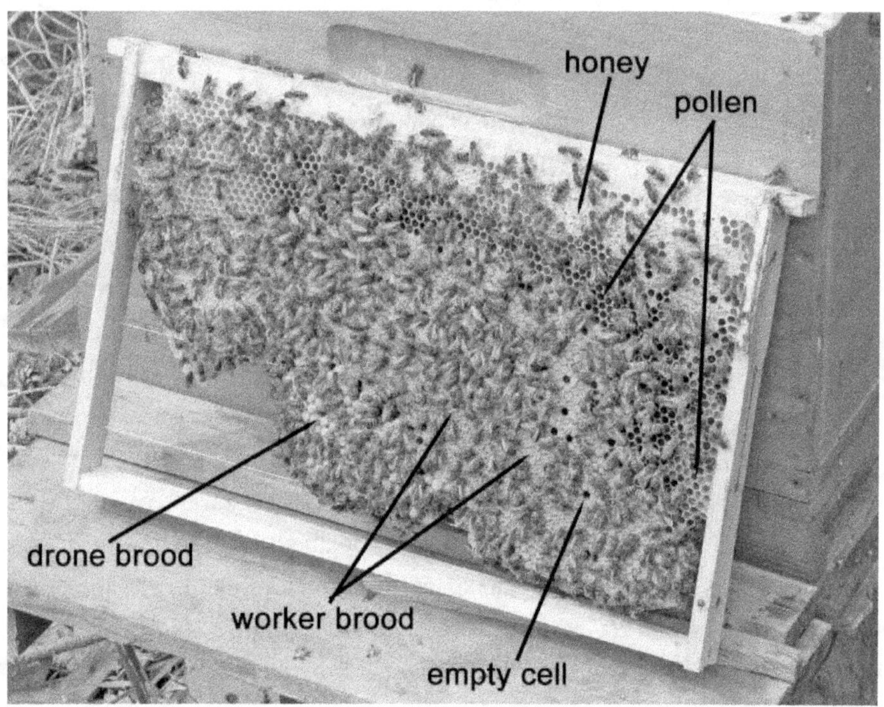

5. Queen excluder: The mother excluder's main responsibilities include gathering pollen, tending to the offspring, and keeping the brood nest enclosed. Fewer than fifty percent of beekeepers employ this affordable piece of equipment. Prior to erecting the excluder, let the bees begin storing nectar in the supers in order to lessen this issue. Bees will be lured to nectar in a pulled comb, which will encourage them to move the excluder. Never place base supers on top of a queen excluder.

A thin covering of plastic or metal that has been perforated with enough holes for personnel to pass through is called an excluder. Round-wire grills that are welded and supported by wooden or metal supports are one type of variation.

A built-in shield of honey frames in the super just above the brood chamber or comb sections keeps the queen in check. Queen excluders are therefore frequently utilized, with the initial supers inserted (again, only installed after any nectar has been deposited in the supers) and subsequently withdrawn. A queen excluder can assist in making sure that brood combs are kept apart from honeycombs to avoid the honey being overly darkened since the beeswax comb used for brooding darkens with use.

In addition, queen excluders are utilized in two-queen schemes to keep queens apart, gather queens in colonies owned by queens, and prevent emergency swarming.

Moreover, an excluder can aid in locating the queen. After three days, if an excluder is placed between two hive bodies, you may determine which hive body is home to the queen by determining the location of the eggs.

6. Inner cover - The highest mega's outer telescopic mask is covered by and underneath the inner cover. The bees are prevented from attaching the mega's outer coat by employing propolis and wax instead of this. Just beneath the outer shell, it provides additional air space for separation. The inner shield protects the interior of the hive from the powerful sun's beams during hot weather. This prevents wintertime moisture-laden air from coming into direct contact with frigid surfaces. If you want to aid extricate bees from full honey supers, you can add a porter bee escape to the center hole in the inner cover.

7. External covering - A telescopic shield on the outside protects the hive sections from the elements. This fits over the inner lid and the top edge of the topmost hive body. To stop weathering and leaks, the roof is typically covered with a layer of metal. Removing the outer cover while leaving the inner cover in place allows the beekeeper to easily smoke the bees prior to the colony being infiltrated and disturbs fewer bees inside the hive.

A translucent cover, sometimes known as a migratory hat, is used by beekeepers who frequently relocate their hives. The sides of the hive body may or may not extend over the ends, and this type of lid sits flush with those sides. These coatings necessitate stacking of colonies in addition to being lightweight and easy to remove. To keep a load on a truck, tight stacking is required.

8. Additional apparatus - In addition to the basic hive components, additional equipment can be added individually. Slatted bottom boards are popular among beekeepers; some are painted in an English pattern. Beekeeping offers a lot of room for creativity and customization.

9. Painting the hive's components: Paint should be applied to all of the hive's exposed exterior surfaces. The hive shouldn't be painted inside since the bees would varnish it with propolis, which is a wax and plant sap mixture. The main goal of painting is to preserve the wood. Most beekeepers utilize external latex or wax-based white paint, which is long-lasting. Having a light color helps prevent heat buildup in the hive during the summer. Different color variants can assist lessen colonial drift, even though white is a typical color.

10. Plastic tools: In the past, redwood, oak, or cypress were used to make the hive's major components. These days, both hive components are offered in plastic.

The plastic frames and hive's snap-together parts are lightweight, sturdy, dependable, simple to assemble, and low maintenance.

Although plastic frames and flooring are more widely used, plastic hive bodies, bottom boards, and coverings have not shown to be as effective since plastic cannot breathe and does not permit rapid moisture ventilation.

Drawing a base is challenging since even plastic warps easily and some forms let in too much light.

11. Suppliers of equipment: New bee equipment is often "knocked down," or unassembled, when it is acquired; however, assembled kits are available for a premium cost and delivery charge. Bee supply vendors will typically include easy-to-follow assembly instructions with their products. It is strongly recommended that beginning beekeepers attempt to install the hive components with the assistance of a more experienced apiarist. To paint their hives before the bees come, novice beekeepers will buy their supplies in advance.

It is best not to place foundation sheets in the frames until it is appropriate since the wax can expand and distort due to storage and handling temperatures, which can lead to poorly drawn combs.

A lot of beekeepers think they can cut costs by building their own gear or by buying secondhand equipment. For every approach, the appliances will be standard ones. When creating beekeeping equipment, a thorough understanding of bee space is essential. You can easily obtain building designs that are accessible or make models out of industrial components. Although the frames require more effort and time, many beekeepers believe they can economically construct bottom boards, hive heads, and roofs. Success is contingent upon the caliber and cost of the materials, the availability of the required equipment, and the beekeeper's proficiency with carpentry.

It is not advisable for novices to purchase old equipment since it can be problematic. Finding a source for used machinery and determining its value or significance can be challenging at first. Additionally, despite being stored for a long time, used equipment may not be the right size or may be contaminated with microorganisms that cause a variety of diseases in bees. In order to verify that the state apiary inspector has examined the hives and found no indications of sickness, kindly request a certificate of inspection.

Regarding beekeeping supplies and equipment, consult to the appendix's list of vendors, state and regional beekeeping directories, the county extension office in your area, national and international beekeeping journals, or the MARC website (maarec.cas.psu.edu).

12. Smoker Ancillary Equipment: A hive and a bee smoker are necessary for operating bees. Smoker size is a personal preference.

The 4 x 7-inch scale is maybe the biggest one used. Considering purchasing or using a smoker with a heat barrier surrounding the firebox to protect yourself and your clothing when you assist the smoker in between your knees during colony operations. Some beekeepers like the type with a hook so they can hang the smoker over the open hive body and yet have it available when inspecting it.

To produce copious amounts of dense, clear smoke, coals must be above the grate and unburned products above the coals. Bark, dried leaves, cotton rags, burlap, corn cobs, wood shavings, pine needles, plastic, punk wood, bark, and sumac bobs are all suitable materials for smokers.

If conditions are right and stealing is not possible, sprinkling sugar syrup and smoke works well. An alternative liquid smoke is available that you mix with water and spray on the bees using a mister-type device.

A metal bar called a "hive tool" is essential for breaking apart the frames of a brood chamber or honey super, extracting the hive bodies, and scraping away propolis and wax from holsters to collect hive equipment. To make the hive tool accessible and keep their fingers safe when lifting boxes to frames, beekeepers frequently hold the tool in the palm of their hands. Propolis, wax, and honey extraction from beehives requires periodic washing. The device can be literally poked into the ground or fried in a smoker's fire bowl to accomplish this; both methods help to prevent the spread of bee illnesses. A putty knife or screwdriver is not a suitable substitute for a strong hive tool and could harm the hive body or frame.

Wear protective clothing: To protect your face and neck from bee stings, you will also be wearing a bee scarf. Three types of veils are commonly available: ones with an opening at the top to conceal a hat, ones that are completely hatless, and ones that are a component of a bee suit. The best protection is provided by wearing a lightweight, wide-brimmed, snugly fitting hat over a wire or cloth veil that protrudes from the face. While they are portable and easily folded for travel, masks without caps don't often fit on the head as snugly as they should. The veil falls across your face and scalp as a result of the elastic band around your head acting backward as you bend forward to deal with bees.

Beekeepers can choose from an extensive selection of coveralls, or bee suits, at varying pricing points. Not all bee suits are created equal and may not always be the safest or easiest to use. If handled carefully and washed often, coveralls can help reduce stings and the likelihood of propolis getting on clothing. Coveralls and shirtveils—long shirts with removable veils attached— are frequently used by beekeepers.

Wearing brown or white clothing is more appropriate for working bees. While many colors are acceptable, dark hues, delicate materials, and clothing made of animal fibers are not well received by bees. Although ripstop nylon coveralls and windbreakers are great for working bees, they can be too heavy to wear in the summer.

Wearing rubber gloves or cloth is advised for beginners who are allergic to stings. A lot of seasoned beekeepers find it inconvenient to use gloves and would rather receive a few stings to facilitate handling. Gloves with a form-fitting design, such ones used for household tasks or laboratory work, reduce stings from honey and propolis and sticky fingers. Bites can occur in dark, socked knees and unprotected wrists. Since ankles are at the hive's entrance, they are also the first target of enraged bees. To keep your pant legs safe, tuck them inside your shoes or boots or secure them with cord or rubber bands. They are tying open shirtsleeves with wristlets, Velcro, or elastic bands to lessen stings on these sensitive spots.

You should refrain from using colognes, perfumes, and aftershave lotions when working with bees since they will attract untrusting bees. To prevent sting or hive scents that could draw or aggravate bees during the examination, regularly launder the gloves and clothing you use.

A Simple Beekeeping Colony

The species of honey bees are gregarious and live in colonies. 20,000–80,000 female workers, hundreds of male drones, and a single queen make up a honey bee colony. Eggs, larvae, and pupae make up every province of honey bees.

Seasonal variations mostly determine the number of individuals inside a colony of honey bees. However, this population will substantially decrease during the colder seasons.

Because every bee caste has a distinct job to do, honey bee colonies depend on population variety to survive. Because drones and workers are necessary to establish new colonies that supply food, fertilizer, and wax for constructing hives, even though queens are extremely powerful individuals within their cultures, they are unable to do so on their own.

Transformation, Every honey bee in a colony goes through the embryonic, larval, and pupal stages of development before becoming an adult. Legless grubs that feed on pollen, nectar, or honey are the larvae of honey bees. Before they reach the pupal stage, caterpillars molt and shed their skin a few times.

These pupae will molt again and emerge as adult honey bees, carrying out intricate tasks for the colony.

Only queens are capable of laying fertile eggs within their colonies. A large honey bee colony depends on having an egg-laying queen that may produce up to 2,000 eggs in a single day. Early in life, queens mate and carry millions of sperm inside of them. They usually survive two to three years while producing eggs, though they can live up to five years.

Workers The majority of honey bees in a colony are those that are employed there.

Although worker bees are entirely female, they are unable to lay fertile eggs. In the absence of a queen, they frequently deposit male drone eggs that have not been fertilized.

In order to defend the colony, worker bees stab their victims with their barbed stingers, which attach to their skin and sever the stinging bee's abdomen, killing it.

Employees are essential honey bee colony representatives. They gather pollen and nectar, tend to drones and queens, lay eggs, ventilate the hive, guard the nest, and take care of the colony in various ways. The life cycle of a worker bee typically lasts six weeks.

Making new queens pregnant is the sole responsibility of drones, or male honey bees. Drones often perish soon after mating and slumber in midair outside. Some honey bee colonies during the fall will expedite surviving drones if there is little food for the colony.

Swarms of Swarming by honey bees is a normal aspect of colony expansion. Because of congestion, honey bees swarm within their hives. In order to produce a swarm, an old honey bee queen will depart the colony with roughly half of the worker bees, while a new queen will remain with the bulk of the workers in the old hive. In the humid hours of the day, in late spring and early summer, honey bees frequently swarm the woodland. Beekeepers work to reduce the frequency of swarming in farmed bees, despite the fact that it is a normal element of a honey bee colony's steady life cycle.

A swarm of honey bees consists of one queen and hundreds or thousands of worker bees. Honey bees are temporarily swarming; they float and eventually land on bushes and tree branches. The clusters spend a few hours to several days resting there, depending on the surroundings and the time it takes to choose a new nesting place. As soon as a Scout honey bee finds a good spot for the new colony, the swarm quickly takes off for the new location.

Swarms of honey bees rarely cause harm to people. Honey bees that are swarming during a crowd have less motivation to attack because they do not have any offspring or a nest to protect.

But when it does, workers may try to protect their queen, and when that happens, a swarm of bees may attack. You will need to hire a pest control expert to either remove or eradicate a huge swarm of bees if they appear in your yard or house. A certified pest management professional should be consulted before taking any independent action because honey bees are a protected species in some areas.

The decision of which strain or breed

Of bee to acquire, and from whom to order it, presents a challenge for novice beekeepers when packing packages and collecting queens.

The variety of honey bee species found in the United States is a result of their importation from Europe, the Middle East, and Africa. Italians,

Caucasians, and Carniolans are the three primary breeds. However, the races that exist in the United States today are distinct from the original races that gave rise to their names.

To determine which breed or strain of bees will best suit your needs, weigh the benefits and disadvantages of growing first. With time, you could want to look for Queens and products from different suppliers and breeders of Queens, and you should educate yourself on the traits and viability of each strain in your location.

Italian bees are the most prevalent breed in the United States. The original black or German bee that the early colonists had brought with them was essentially supplanted by them when they were first introduced in 1859. The abdomen of the Italian bee has contrasting black and brown markings, giving it a gray or light yellowish color. People who have three gastric bands (workers) are commonly called leather-colored Italians; people who have five groups are sometimes called cordovan queens or goldens. Large colonies are produced by Italian bees during the active season, since they seem to start breeding early in the spring and continue until late October. In a comparatively short time, large colonies can gather significant volumes of nectar. However, they also require more honey for upkeep in the fall and winter than do the dark races. Calm and mild on the combs are the majority of Italian bee strains. The disadvantages include a lower ability to coordinate than other species, which causes more bees to stray from colony to colony, and a greater inclination to steal, which may contribute to the spread of disease. It turned out that the Italians were skilled housekeepers.

The main cause of the replacement of black bees with European foulbrood (EFB) is the relative immunity of Italians to it. The Italian queen is more difficult to locate in the hive than the queens of the other two species because of her paler coloring. The brilliant white caps that the Italian bees produce are ideal for extracting honey from the nest.

Caucasian honey bees are sometimes referred to as the softest bee species. Their abdomens have grayish stripes and are dark to black in color.

They utilize a ton of propolis to lower the entrance height and fasten combs, and they prefer to make burr combs. Nevertheless, fewer propolis is used in some of the older kinds. Because of their enormous proposal, they are not deemed appropriate for the production of comb honey. Though they won't overcrowd, Caucasians are prone to stray and rob.

Store honey for a little while longer than the Italians, as colonies typically don't reach their peak until the middle of the summer. We frequently feed in significantly colder climates than Italian bees, and there is evidence of some resistance to EFB. Though they are not many, Caucasians do exist.

Carniolans are black bees with white dots or bands on their abdomen, resembling the color of Caucasians. These bees overwinter as little clusters, but once the first pollen is available in the spring, they grow quickly.

But unnecessary swarming is the biggest negative. They possess a strong sense of direction, are composed on the combs, and are unlikely to cheat.

Though inaccessible, they exist. Some beekeepers believe that this stock is the best of its kind, even though the majority of it is categorized as new world colonianes.

Honey bees from different lines or races were combined to generate hybrid bees.

A variety of extremely productive bees with what is known as hybrid vigor are also produced by initially planned crossings. Matings under guidance can maintain this vitality. Crossing inbred lines that have been selected and kept for certain qualities like smoothness, profitability, or wintering results in commercial hybrids like Midnite and Starline.

Over time, a variety of bee strains from southwest England were selected to create the breed known as buckfast bees. They adapt better to the chilly climate of the area and are more resistant to tracheal mites. The supply, which includes sperm, semen, and adult queens, was brought into the United States and is easily accessible. It came from Canada.

Researchers and queen breeders are experimenting with immune-compliant bees in response to the devastating effects of drug-resistant illnesses and parasitic mites. Now, any of these stockpiles will be bought as royalty. As stock selected for more northern regions gained appeal, so did the demand for it. The Ohio Buckeye variety is one option. Under West Virginian conditions, these bees exhibit all the characteristics of truly superb bees, including exceptional resistance to tracheal mites.

Bees belonging to other stock groups, such Russian, SMR, or Hybrid (also called Minnesota hybrid), are chosen based on their enhanced mite resistance and better hygienic practices, like as cleaning the hive by removing dead or dying brood. This characteristic makes bees more efficient at eliminating potentially dangerous viruses from their hive. If you have any doubts about the statements made about the stock's qualities, it is advisable to ask your possible supplier, just like you should with any stock. It is a good idea to see what other beekeepers have experienced with the stock.

The various breeds of bees that are adapted to different parts of the world are the result of natural selection. Bees are not particularly well suited to contemporary beekeeping because of their naturally selected traits. Within the area, there are also other racial groups. The Western Hemisphere only received a small number. We shall examine the notable varieties that are obtainable in North America and discuss their usefulness in producing comb honey in these temperate regions.

There are benefits to both types of bees for beekeeping. However, every species of bee also possesses negative traits. These particular characteristics can promote or hinder honeycomb development. A lot of races show varying degrees of interest depending on where they live. Different regions have different cycles for the production of pollen and the dispersion of nectar.

Which bee species are more suitable for your area should be carefully considered. When the objective is to comb the production of honey, the judgment is most crucial.

Apismelliferascutellata: The evolution of the bee population in some parts of North America now incorporates African bee DNA. The most detrimental effect on the growth of comb honey is typically not violent defensive behavior. The capacity to swarm or escape is significantly greater in Africanized bees. A fresh bundle of bees might leave the hive after clearly accepting a new body. After a month of residency, Africanized bees will depart from the brood and relocate to a new hive. This activity was extremely uncommon, if not nonexistent, prior to African genetics becoming known in the Western Hemisphere.

Fall will see a swarm of African genetically modified bees. This action was extremely uncommon or nonexistent prior to the Africanization of our bees. Additionally, a lot of bees have been more aggressively protective than others. Africanized Bees elevate this characteristic to a completely new level. In African history, bees were not robbed under the Sahara. The single targets that bee criminals will first select include bees that have been stolen by locals, as well as honey badgers and other African animals. They will next select offensive or defensive tactics. The only drawback is that compared to European races, Africans typically have a different control over the Varroa destructor.

The Italian honey bee breed, Apismelliferaligustica, has historically been the most prevalent bee in our country. Certain Italian bees have advantages as well.

Italian bees are primarily more competitive than other species. Italians are already hibernating for the winter across most of our nation. They typically raise their young before other breeds. Compared to other species, this one doesn't swarm very often.

Italian bees are often less aggressive than most other species. An important benefit for those who develop honeycomb is that Italian bees have a long history of using propolis. Drones are banished from the Italian colony during the early season. If at all, they will swarm late in the season.

Bees from Italy can have unwelcome apps. This type of bee is more likely to steal than others. They'll rapidly destroy less powerful colonies. In colder climates, they don't overwinter as much as other races do. Italian provinces employ a greater number of markets, thus they require greater feeding or have a higher honey content than other species. Italian bees can continue to produce offspring even when the nectar flow stops, provided that a baby is accessible. More drones than other caste colonies will be found in the Italian colony. If the brood of stored honey or feed begins to increase, winter losses with Italian bees may be larger.

This bee's new spring build-up traits make it suited for honey production in temperate forest regions. This includes much of the United States, stretching from the Ozark Plain east to the Atlantic Ocean.

Of all the North American breeds available, Italian bees might be your best bet if your primary honey production is produced in April and May.

The Italian bees on our continent have bred themselves into hygienic habits. Its two main goals are to stop infections and control mites.

The growth of comb honey requires the largest honey flow, regardless of race. Early in the season is usually when your best flow occurs, so Italian bees will probably be ready soon and will benefit from the early honey flood. Trees often blossom early in the spring. In February, maple trees bloom in this part of the nation.

Apismelliferacaucasica: A amiable bee native to the Caucasus. The most endearing butterfly is the reason for its fame. White people don't work in the downturn. Though they don't swarm as much as other races, this bee creates healthy colonies. Not every aspect of those bees is ideal. It is fabled that they use propolis. They practically barricade the hive's entrance. In the colony, blocks can be challenging to break apart. Regular labor is necessary if you wish to lose the frames at all. A later honey flow or faster run is preferred by the Caucasian bee, who is hesitant to build up. The Caucasian population poses a threat to Nosema.

The honey cappings of Caucasians are square and they produce less honey. Compared to other bee races, Caucasians have a higher likelihood of migrating.

Establishing the Bee Colony

A large component of many ecosystems is made up of bees. Many species depend on bees for pollination of plants, and in recent years, concerns about bee population declines have heightened fears of a significant loss of biodiversity and of predating bees' blossoming insect nests. It provides a nutritional commodity in the form of honey in addition to the benefit of maintaining the species permanently on the ground to carry out the necessary tasks of pollination.

Talk with Others Prior to starting your beekeeping journey, you must confer with four different groups of people. First and foremost, your family. Keeping bees in the garden would require everyone's approval. Secondly, remember to confer with the physician. While it might seem strange to seek medical advice for a permaculture project, a small percentage of individuals are allergic to bee stings, and getting bitten can have serious health consequences. To find out if you or any family members are at risk, a doctor can perform a simple test. Consult your neighbors second. Someone else might object to or react negatively to being near bees. Beekeeping at your location can be prohibited by zoning regulations.

Locate a Site Similar to any other species, you must locate a location that will satisfy all of your bees' requirements. To provide them with food, you want a lot of plants close by.

They also need to have access to a swimming pool. To ensure the hive works for as long as possible, place it in broad light. However, protect the hive from strong gusts, as they may overturn the hive and scatter the colony. Perhaps pick a spot where there is high fencing and lots of trees around. The result is that the bees soar higher than a human's height. You'll need to work with the hive on a frequent basis, so eventually place it somewhere you can easily access it.

To make a stand, beehives should be maintained at a high altitude. This keeps air flowing through the hive and keeps ground predators from invading the colony. A elevated hive is even more advantageous for permaculture gardeners as it eliminates the need to bend over in order to tend to the colony. With a wooden pallet placed on top, old concrete blocks provide a great platform for bee hives.

Putting Up a Hive Beehives are made up of several sheets of beeswax that are suspended vertically inside a shell. At least two sheet rates exist in the hive; the bees store their honey on the top sheet rate, while they gather their young on the bottom sheet rate.

A tier enclosure with racked frames to hang the beeswax sheets will need to be made or purchased. If you want to build your own hive, you might be able to purchase one from another beekeeper or use repurposed materials.

Possessing any apparatus A start-up investment is required for beekeeping. The bare minimal amount of equipment required is a smoker and a hood. To keep bees from getting into your hair or stinging exposed parts of your face, the hood comes with a hat and a scarf that hangs below the neck or is fastened. Though you might be able to create your own, get advice from an experienced beekeeper to make sure you are well covered.

Once you get the hang of handling bees, a hood will suffice, however initially you might feel more inclined to acquire a complete body suit with boots and gloves. Again, let other beekeepers in the neighborhood know if they have any used suits they'd like to get rid of.

One essential piece of equipment for handling bees is the smoker. Whenever you wish to perform some work for the hive, you pump wood (rotted wood should work as well, but pine needles work well) into the container using a bottle with a bellows attached. The bees' chemical messages to one another are confused by the smoke, making them more confused and disturbed. As a result, they leave you alone to conduct any necessary study.

Purchase some hives. After your hive is assembled, it's time to store it. Accredited organic suppliers are the source of the colonies. Three species are commonly found. Easy to manage, Italian bees produce a large amount of honey. Although Carniolan bees are resilient and can withstand even extremely cold winters, Russian bees are likewise docile but can be less productive in the early spring.

Offering the opportunity to host a problematic colony is an option to purchasing bees. To keep an eye out for pests, kindly get in touch with the local beekeepers. When a bee colony is called in to remove itself from an inappropriate place, such as the eaves of a nursing home or a school playground, you may give the bees a fresh lease on life rather than eliminating them. Additionally, the colony's presence anyplace close is a sign that it has acclimated to the climate and can find enough food to survive in the area.

Keep in mind that if you are starting a new colony, the hive might not produce enough extra honey for you to harvest in the first year. That is when the province's population grows. Even before then, though, the bees will play a crucial role in your permaculture ecosystem and you will be able to harvest some honey by year two.

The Colony and Its Establishment

Since honey bees are social insects, their large, well-kept communities of families are their home. Unlike the majority of solitary insects, social insects are highly specialized and engage in a variety of intricate tasks. To effectively exist in social colonies, honey bees have evolved a variety of behaviors, including labor division, communication, complex nest-building, environmental preservation, and security. In general, social insects—and honey bees specifically—are among the newest creatures on Earth because of their interesting activities.

The three adult worker groups that make up a honey bee colony are typically laborers, drones, and a queen. Worker bees in their thousands work together to build nests, collect food, and raise larvae. — based on their mature age, the participant has a specific role to fulfill. However, the colony's entire collective effort is needed for life and reproduction. Individual bees, including workers, drones, and queens, are dependent on the colony for survival.

Between late spring and summer, a colony typically consists of thousands of worker adults, a single queen, and several hundred drones (Figure 1). The queen and workers' presence, which depends on an effective communication network, sustains the social order of the colony. The communication "dances" and the spread of chemical pheromones among members are responsible for keeping an eye on the activities necessary for colony survival. Worker bee labor methods are mostly determined by age, though they can also change depending on the demands of the colony. The size of the working force, the quantity of food storage, and the queen all affect how frequently the population reproduces and settles. The productivity of the colony increases as its size grows, reaching a maximum of 60,000 workers.

Queen

There is just one queen per colony, either following swarming arrangements or over a different period of time. She is the only female who has undergone sexual evolution, hence her main function is reproduction. She gives birth to both fertilized and unfertilized eggs. The majority of Queens' egg production occurs in the spring and early summer. When they are at their most developed, queens can lay up to 1,500 eggs every day. Their egg-laying gradually stops in early October, and they don't lay many eggs until early January of the following year. Up to 250,000 eggs and perhaps more than a million eggs can be produced annually by a single queen.

A queen is easily recognized from the other colony members. She often has a much longer physique than a worker or drone, especially during the egg-laying cycle when her abdomen grows significantly longer.

The workers' and drones' folded arms nearly reach the tip of the abdomen, while her wings barely cover roughly two-thirds of the stomach. A queen lacks both functional wax glands and pollen baskets, and her thorax is slightly larger than a worker's. Although her barbs are shorter and smaller than the worker's, her stinger is curved and longer. The usual length of the queen's active life is two to three years, but she can live up to five years at a time.

A queen's primary function also involves producing pheromones, which act as a social "glue," binding a colony of bees together and contributing to their unique character. Although Termed Queen Substance is the main pheromone produced by her mandibular glands, other pheromones are also vital. The queen's ability to produce eggs and digest chemicals has a significant impact on the quality of the colony. The effectiveness, height, and disposition of the colony are greatly influenced by her genetic composition as well as the drones she is mating with.

After emerging from a queen-cell, the queen spends about a week leaving the hive to mate with other drones in flight. The first one circles the hive to get her bearings because she has to travel a distance to mat from her colony (a natural method of preventing inbreeding). She is barely thirteen minutes away when she departs the hive on her own. Usually in the afternoon, at a height of more than twenty feet, the Queen mates with seven to fifteen drones. The queen's chemical scent, or pheromone, will help drones recognize and recall her. The queen can only lay unfertilized eggs that will eventually develop into drones if inclement weather prevents her from mating for longer than twenty days. Within 48 hours of mating, the queen returns to the hive to start laying eggs. That some sperm are released from the spermatheca when she deposits an egg that will either become a worker or a queen. Her egg will not develop into sperm unless it is placed in a cell that is larger than a helicopter's.

The colony's worker bees never stop tending to the queen, who also gets fed royal jelly. The queen will lay a certain number of eggs, determined by her food intake and the size of the worker who will create the beeswax cells for her eggs and tend to the larvae that will hatch in three days. The staff intends to remove the queen (supersede) when the queen's secreted substance is no longer sufficient. It is possible for the new queen and the old queen to remain in the hive after supersedure for a while.

Fertilized eggs or young worker larvae give rise to new (virgin) queens that are no older than three days. There are three distinct situations in which new queens are raised: swarming, supersedure, and emergency. The larvae of younger workers are chosen by the bees to create queens in an emergency when a previous queen is inadvertently killed, lost, or ejected. These queens are vertically positioned on top of the comb during birth, in worker cells that have been altered (Figure 2). The colony is getting ready to raise a new queen when an older queen begins to suffer (decreased queen material output). Because they get more nourishment (royal jelly) throughout production, queens generated as a result of supersedure are usually superior to queens of urgency. The supersedure queen cells are typically positioned above the emergency queen cells, which resemble combs. The queen cells that are created in advance of swarming, on the other hand, are found in the gaps in the brood area of the beeswax combs or along the lower edges of the plates.

Unmanned Aerial Systems

Largest bees in the colony are called drones (male bees). Usually, you can only find them in late spring and summer. The drone's head is far bigger than the worker's or queen's, and his compound eyes meet at the top of his head. Pollen sacks, stingers, or wax glands are absent from drones.

Their vital function is to induce fertilization in the virgin queen while she is in flight for mating. Drones develop, take around a week to reach sexual maturity, and die right away after mating. Since the drones don't accomplish anything beneficial for the hive, it is thought that normal colony activity depends on their presence.

Even though they usually depend on food workers, drones can start feeding themselves within the hive after they turn four days old. The food supply in the colony will be under more stress if there are a lot of drones because they eat three times as much as people do. After they are about eight days old, the drones remain in the hive until they take flights for orientation. Typically, hive flight occurs between noon and 4:00 p.m. We have never witnessed drones harvesting fruit's blossoms. Drones usually are tossed outside into the cold and left to starve to death when fall brings chilly weather and a shortage of pollen and nectar sources. They must, however, remain in the hive permanently in Queenless Colonies.

Workers

Most workers who occupy a colony are workers, who are the smallest. These are underdeveloped sexually and do not deposit eggs under typical hive circumstances. A large portion of the hive's work is carried out by workers thanks to their intricate systems, which include pollen sacks, smell, wax, and brood food glands. Incoming nectar is handled, the cells are cleaned and polished, the brood is cooked, the queen is looked after, garbage is cleared out, beeswax combs are constructed, the entry and air filter are guarded, and the hive is ventilated as an adult during its first few weeks. Later on, when they are field bees, they gather nectar, pollen, water, and propolis (plant sap).

The summertime life cycle of a worker lasts roughly six weeks. As they can live up to six months, workers raised in the fall help the colony survive the winter and procreate until they perish in the spring.

Putting Workers to Rest Many workers' ovaries grow until a colony is queenless and the workers start laying unfertilized eggs. The involvement of the queen, brood, and their chemical constituents is thought to impede the growth of the workers' ovaries. When workers participate in a colony, the province usually loses its queen for a period of one or two weeks. But in ordinary "queenright" colonies, laying workers are also visible during the swarming season and when an unruly queen is in charge of the province. Small-bodied drones are raised in cells the size of workers, and colonies of lay workers are easily identified because there can be five to fifteen eggs per cell anyplace (Figure 3). Furthermore, eggs can be found on the sides of cells instead of at the base, where a queen typically deposits them, and laying workers distribute their eggs more evenly throughout the brood combs. A portion of these eggs do not hatch, and many of the drone larvae that do hatch in the smaller cells do not reach adulthood.

Development of bees All three adult forms of honey bees go through the embryo, larva, and pupa developmental phases before they emerge as adults.

The three phases of grief are a widely used term. While the stages of growth are the same, they are not all the same length (see Table 1). While fertilized eggs can develop into workers or queens, unfertilized eggs become drones.

Female bee caste formation is heavily influenced by nutrition; worker-destined larvae receive less royal jelly and more of a honey-pollen mixture than the large volumes of royal jelly that the queen larva collects.

Rooster Eggs The queen of honey bees typically lays one egg per cell. The developing egg, which resembles a tiny grain of rice, is affixed to the cell's bottom. When first placed, the egg lays squarely atop the end (Figure 4).

On the other hand, during the three-day growth cycle, the egg begins to turn over. The larval stage comes to a conclusion on the third day when the egg hatches into a little grub.

Larvae Safe larvae have a shimmering, pearly white coloring.

They form a "C" when bent to the bottom of the cell (Figure 5). After the larvae are around 5 1/2, 6, and 6 1/2 days old, respectively, job cells, queen cells, and drone cells are capped. As larvae, they are fed by adult worker bees, or nurse bees, while they are still within their beeswax cells. The stage that follows the battery's capping is known as the prepupal level. The larva continues to resemble a grub at this point, but it has begun to stretch lengthwise within the cell and spin a thin silk cocoon. Larvae stay bright white, plump, and shiny during the prepupal stage.

Pupas Within each individual cell, the prepupae continue to change from larval to adult bees, with the help of adult worker bees who supply a beeswax cover (Figure 6). Stable pupae in the early stages of development tend to have bodies more like those of adults, but they still look white and shiny. The first characteristic to start changing color is compound eyes, which go from white to a brownish-purple hue. Not long later, the remainder of the body begins to resemble an adult bee. Within 12, 7, 1, 1/2, and 14, 1/2 days following the capping of their cells, new workers, queens, and drones appear, respectively.

Patterns of brooding The capped brood makes it simple to identify healthy brood patterns. When the queen skips a few cells during the egg-laying process, right-capped worker brood frames typically follow a clear pattern. The caps are free of punctures, convex, and have a medium brown tint. Due of their developmental stage, drone broods typically occur in patches along the pebble's edges, with four times as many pupae and half as many larvae as eggs.

The Hive

Not very hard, are beehives. In their houses, skilled craftspeople construct their own stores. The may hive essentially requires a roof or an external cover.

A protective shield located directly beneath the roof serves the primary purpose of preventing bees from adhering the roof to the upper edges of the hive box situated beneath it. Although having an inside cover is not absolutely necessary, this is nevertheless a valuable piece of equipment.

A configuration of supers and hive bodies determined by the yearly season is found beneath the inner layer. When a queen has no unit, many beekeepers confine her to the brood room or chambers. In a typical springtime hive, things like two supers and two hive bodies will be in good condition. A bottom board gives the colony an advantage by providing a landing spot for bees beneath all the different boxes that are being used. A hive stand often provides protection for the entire beehive system.

A large hammer will be required to join the heavy hive parts after first using a tiny hammer or brad nailer to assemble the frames.

Many novice beekeepers already own part of the required equipment because the majority of hive equipment is constructed of wood. When installing hive components, a variety of minor shop equipment can be helpful, including hammers, a couple of chisels, pliers for cutting damaged nails, and a couple of pipe clamps.

You'll definitely want a bottle of regular external glue for different joints in the frame sections and hive equipment.

A location for hive assembly might be found close to anyplace. Use whatever you have; most beekeepers work in workshops or similar settings.

A properly equipped wood store is not necessary, although having a small compressor and a pneumatic brad nailer are useful tools that aren't absolutely necessary.

The hive components seen in this magnified view of the hive are those found in a typical beehive. When constructing hive equipment at home, it is imperative to adopt conventional dimensions.

The hive components seen in this magnified view of the hive are those found in a typical beehive. When constructing hive equipment at home, it is imperative to adopt conventional dimensions.

Types of joints found in beekeeping equipment While some homemade boxes are constructed with simple butt joints, the two most prevalent hive joints seen in traditional wood hive equipment are box joints and die joints.

Provided joints, whether purchased commercially or from a home store, are slightly more difficult to assemble than box joints but are easier to construct.

Now is the time to put the pipe pin clamps discussed before to use. These are useful for assembly of the disassembled parts and for temporarily holding the pieces in place until the final steps of gluing and nailing are completed.

Beehive ceilings The outermost covering of the hive could be totally plastic or coated in metal. Transparent covers for flat boards are a common tool used by experienced beekeepers. Usually, amateur beekeepers employ the telescoping metal covering hive top. Although it is not a common occurrence, hive tops can occasionally fly off in high winds. In order to prevent this uncommon occurrence, beekeepers occasionally place a weight on top of the hive.

Typically, wooden hive tops with wire coatings are used by hobby beekeepers. Painting a wooden hive cover with a rim should be done on a regular basis to prevent rotting from moisture and rain. A more affordable, simpler, and nonetheless functional top is a flat board cover. Although they essentially require no care, plastic coverings can bend or bow. Over time, the extended polystyrene toppers and plastic would both continue to deteriorate. Ironically, temperature-related degradation can be prevented with chemical painting equipment.

Typically, wooden hive tops with wire coatings are used by hobby beekeepers. Painting a wooden hive cover with a rim should be done on a regular basis to prevent rotting from moisture and rain. A more affordable, simpler, and nonetheless functional top is a flat board cover. Although they essentially require no care, plastic coverings can bend or bow. Over time, polystyrene stretched heads and plastic can both continue to degrade. It's ironic that chemical painting supplies can prevent damage brought on by warmth.

Essential but auxiliary hive equipment is found within coverings and queen excluders. To make propolis, a material used by bees, some colony experts harvest natural rosin from trees and occasionally bushes. Using this simple glue, the bees should be able to securely glue the parts of the hive together. Without an inside cover, the bees will cling tightly to the top box. Often, pounding on the beehive will agitate the bees and cause them to release it.

The queen excluder serves a somewhat different purpose but has the same external dimensions as the inner mask. In order to push the queen to fit through the network, the metal grid is specifically made to allow worker bees to pass through. The queen is confined to a specific section of the hive in this manner, mixing brood with the honey the beekeeper will eventually remove.

The inner cover rests flush against the hive's sides. Indeed, the bees are able to glue it as well, but the beekeeper will use a hive tool with a pointed end to pop it out of the space between the inner cover and the top edge of the shell. If you smash the outermost surface to clean it, guard bees aren't as appetizing as they should be. Keeping the bees quiet is still pleasant. The queen excluder is a very contentious piece of equipment. Many beekeepers think that because of the grid, bees carrying nectar cannot travel across the network. And all the other beekeepers would be without their hives, but for one. Whether you utilize this app or not is entirely up to you.

This is far too common with beekeeping equipment; any kind of bottom board fits incredibly well. During the winter, the screened window can be covered with a metal sheet. Underneath the filtering frame, the sturdy bottom plate gets thicker and more rigid. This model is used by a lot of beekeepers, particularly commercial keepers.

This is far too common with beekeeping equipment; any kind of bottom board fits incredibly well. The screened window can be sealed up in the winter by installing a metal covering. Beneath the filtering frame, the heavy bottom plate thickens and gets stickier. This model is used by a lot of beekeepers, particularly commercial keepers.

The base board, or hive's cornerstone The bottom board is essentially simply a big surface once everything is said and done. For many years, the majority of beekeepers used solid bottom boards with a three-sided rim, but these days, screened bottom boards are very popular. The invasive parasitic Varroa mite, which seriously harms honey bees, is somewhat controlled using screened boards. Ticks are released from the bees and fall to the ground via the screened aperture.

Frame numbers with base inserts that are correct are required for growing bee boxes. The honey storage box, also known as a super, can hold ten frames and twenty deep frames, for example, according to the tables previously indicated. Less frames would presumably be required for the 8-frame equipment.

Frame numbers with base inserts that are correct are required for growing bee boxes. The honey storage box, also known as a super, can hold ten frames and twenty deep frames, for example, according to the tables previously indicated. Less frames would presumably be required for the 8-frame equipment.

Supers and brood boxes are the two primary components of a beehive. This hive is composed of a 65/8" super on top, a white plastic hive body in second place, a designated joint hive body in third place, and a normal box collective hive body on the floor. Since the hardware is all from different sources, it is all essentially compatible. This hive has a 65/8" super on top, followed by a white plastic hive body in second place, a provided joint hive body in third place, and a conventional box collective hive in bottom place. Everything is essentially the same, even the hardware, which is sourced from many vendors.

With a few exceptions, every bee box is the same size, measuring 193½4" long by 1614" wide. The hive's deepest part, which is often utilized as a brood box for bee reproduction, is around 9 1/2" deep. Supers are long, multi-length boxes mostly used for storing sugar. Standard size 65/8" deep supers are used for storing honey.

Yes, there are a few different factors.

Yes, there are a number of variables with hive equipment that need to be addressed first. An rookie beekeeper may find themselves a little disoriented. The feeling will disappear shortly as the procedure becomes uncomplicated and pleasant. Depending on the yearly seasonal nectar flows, different types of hive equipment are required for different beehive setups.

Aside from the bees, what is actually inside the hive?

In reasonable distance. Bee box, often called equipment with ten games, comes with ten sets of combs. Using eight frames, this is the second form of hive hardware that many beekeepers eagerly support; it is also substantially smaller. A base insert with an embossed effect of honey bee cells is coated in wax and attached to each frame. The bees may now make straight wax combs instead of the typical curved combs forming on their own thanks to these implants.

The whole wonder of the beehive is that it keeps "bee space." Wherever in the hive, the bee gap of 1/4-3/8 "is believed to be used to distinguish between component sections, including the tops of the posts, sides, bottom of the container, under the inner cover, and in between the queen excluders. Otherwise, whether the room is bigger or smaller, bees can jam anything using wax or bee glue (propolis). For the modern hive equipment to function properly, there must be bee space between the frames and other parts of the hive.

Why is that not working?

outdated equipment for beekeeping Equipment for beekeeping may be found by a novice beekeeper at auctions or from someone selling used equipment. You could write an entire section in the short-be alert on this subject because there are so many variables. Ask for guidance from your exemplary beekeeper partner, but bear in mind that he might choose to purchase it as well. Standard wax combs should be avoided. They could be unwell. After they publish something like this, beekeepers frequently receive good offers on used items.Once again, be exercised caution.

Top bar hives Top bar hives (TBH) come in a variety of forms and are popular among beekeepers. The original beekeeper should not find it startling to be exposed to these equipment options at such an early age. Even while these hive designs are entertaining and fascinating from a biological standpoint, unless the beginner beekeeper has a TBH mentor, they will be better off starting with normal facilities. Regular equipment use provides the newbie with more assistance and understanding.

Equipment for personal protection In order to handle the bees, the beekeeper would require protective gear, hive devices, and bees to house the bees. There are currently multiple varieties and styles of safety clothes available, just like there are for different kinds of hive hardware.

10.First, an unsightly face mask; second, a half-suite with a veil attached; and third, a full-length suit with a fixed veil, in that order. It is common for inexperienced beekeepers to buy a full-length suit since they are apprehensive about this new profession and are concerned about the occasional sting. With a full set of protective gloves and adjustable clips at the wrists and ankles, there's no way a testy bee will ever discover a weak area to strike. It's sweaty and careless to wear the complete costume, which is the problem with it. However, everything is flawless when beekeeping first starts.

Wear progressively less protective gear as beekeepers' faith grows. However, the novice will see that all experienced beekeepers should exercise considerable caution to ensure they always have a full protective gear on hand for these infrequent bee encounters. This would be an excellent opportunity to outfit bees in their full costume and switch colonies at night.

Feeling protected is the golden rule when it comes to safety gear. You will not become an apiary if you do not work the bees. Do you actually feel secure and at ease wearing a beeswax dress?

All you'll need for this is a smoker and a hive machine. Smoking beehive 9The beehive smoker is practically the industry standard for beekeeping equipment.

Bee colonies are meant to be exposed to bright, fluffy smoke from smokers, which causes some confusion among the bees under observation. The beekeepers depart at that point.

Elderly smokers accumulate a wealth of memories and an old cigarette atmosphere. Bee smokers have the ability to burn almost any type of gasoline, but that's a topic for another debate. A smoker, or smokers, are a requirement for many beekeepers. The majority of proficient beekeepers tend to have a pair. For hive management, this is an essential piece of equipment.

Hive Instrument Recall the propolis, or bee glue, we talked about before. To access and remove frames from a hive, especially after 8–10 months of gluing and waxing bees, would require a hive device, which is essentially a pry bar. Every beekeeper has one beekeeper missing, and both beekeepers occasionally lose one in the wilderness. It wouldn't matter whether you got a few of those necessary items.

Types of Hive & How to Select the Best One for You

For the novice beekeeper, there are numerous hive styles to choose from. Regarding their ideal habitat, give the bees any extra attention.

Naturally, we adore the honey that bees produce, but if we want to retain bees, we also recognize that bees are essential to effective pollination. What kind of hive would be best for us is still up for debate. Various elements that vary throughout beekeepers will determine this conclusion. To assist you in selecting the ideal hive for your crop and yourself, consider these three options.

1. LANGSTROTH HIVE This omnipresent "bee house" is the most popular substitute used by contemporary beekeepers. This was created in 1851 by Massachusetts pastor and hobbyist beekeeper Dr. L. L. Langstroth. It was the first hive with detachable frames, which made it simpler for beekeepers to access the colony for bee inspections. An inner cover, an outer cover, frames, one or two deep supers (181-404 by 141-04 by 91-02), and one or two honey supers make up a Langstroth hive.

Easier Harvesting Benefits: A Langstroth hive has several advantages, but the best part is the honey it produces.

Mobility: Because its components can be disassembled and reassembled, a Langstroth hive is easier to move about than a topbar or Warré hive.

Production: Increasing honey and brood and decreasing drone production are the goals of Langstroth hives. Langstroth hives are a wise choice whether you're raising queens or collecting pollen and propolis.

A major selling point of the Langstroth design is its ventilation, which is essential on hot summer days. Not only does it have better ventilation than a top-bar hive, but it also facilitates bee aggregation in the cold winter months.

Simple to Locate Information: According to the Oregon Master Beekeeper

Program, Langstroth hives might be a better option for novices despite their ease of use and wealth of knowledge.

Drawbacks Weight: Up to 60 pounds is the weight of a deep super fully charged unit! Beekeepers are not the same as weightlifters.

Aesthetics: Langstroth hives don't look natural or attractive, yet because of how often they are viewed, they almost seem invisible.

Unnatural Design: Bees prefer to build combs in tall, circular structures. Because of the Langstroth's rectangular shape, beekeepers frequently have to move outer frames into the center where the bees need them. This causes the bees' work to be disrupted and increases their effort in maintaining the ideal humidity and temperature in the hive. Bees disturb the colony and maintain a particular degree of moisture and temperature, which puts them at danger of infection and encroachment. But there are a lot of tasks for bees and beekeepers to complete.

2. HARRÉ HIVE Even though you are unfamiliar with Warré hives, you are not alone. French priest Emile Warré created the hive model, which is becoming more and more popular in the United States. Warré experimented with and studied many types of hives throughout his life. He created "The People's Hive" in the early 1900s. Comparable in size to a Langstroth hive, the design features square rather than rectangular sections (12 inches wide and 8 inches deep), and the boxes are fastened to the bottom as opposed to the top.

Hands-off Benefits of Beekeeping: Bees construct their comb on foundationless plates in the Warré hive, a vertical variation of the top-bar hive that is designed to resemble a hollow tree and aid colonies in surviving the winter. This design produces happy, stable bees and, of course, reduces the meddling of beekeepers. If pollination is one of your main goals, this is the perfect hive.

Control of Humidity and Temperature: A sawdust insulating box sandwiched between two layers of cotton cloth is placed atop the hive. This structure assists in controlling the temperature and humidity.

Aesthetics: Although rectangular in shape, Warré hives have a less functional appearance. Because of their size and peaked roof design, they can have a very charming appearance in a yard or outdoor space.

Results: Honey output could be on par with a Langstroth method if boxes are inserted on time.

Drawbacks Cost: Compared to Langstroth hives, warré hives can be more expensive if you don't make them yourself. Additionally, the ingredients are harder to get by.

Work for Two: Because Warré hives are constructed from the bottom up, adding supers requires the assistance of a second individual.

Extracting Tools: Since honey-extraction equipment is primarily designed for Langstroth hive frames, extracting honey is more difficult than it is with a Langstroth hive.

No Front Feeder: Because a Warré hive cannot accommodate a front feeder, new technologies may be needed to supplement the colonies as needed.

3. HIVE FOR TOP-BAR Although top-bar hives have been present for many years, in one form or another, they are relatively new in the US. Simplicity is crucial in this situation: Without the use of a plastic base, this kind of hive uses wooden bars suspended over a hive cavity with wax strips added to the underside to encourage comb building. Evidence points to the usage of pots or baskets by Greek beekeepers for this reason.

Common top-bar hives had a roof on the ends and a screened entrance, resembling long, one-story wooden boxes with a small triangle shape on the bottom. To observe the colony in action, some individuals install one side of a plexiglass screen.

benefits

Cost: Building a top-bar hive is simple and requires only a small initial investment.

Hive Access: There are no big supers to deal with, and working the hive is made simpler by the fact that you take frames one at a time, which usually weigh between three and seven pounds.

Preserve Space: With this type of hive, you may simply divide the hive until your colony need more space. You don't need to store any more hive components, such as supers.

Limited Disruptions: When operating a hive with a top-bar configuration, bees encounter minimal disturbances. If pollination is your main goal, this may be the best configuration.

Drawbacks

Temperature control: In cold weather, top-bar hives make it more challenging for bees to regulate their body temperature. A cold snap may decimate colonies more quickly because of the bees' increased difficulty in remaining warm due to the expansive, one-level box structure.

Inconsistent production: It's harder to measure the production of honey than it is for a Langstroth hive. What is your intake? What is your deviation?

Lack of Standardized Equipment: If you are building your own box, it is difficult to get standardized equipment for top-bar hives.

Raising Queens: In a hive like this, raising queens is more difficult since it can be difficult to isolate the active queen.

Whether you maintain bees for honey or pollination is ultimately the most important element in deciding which kind of hive you should build. Consider your time commitment, initial investment, supply availability, back strength, and, ultimately, the health of your colonies while making your decisions about beekeeping. You'll finally be on your way to a fascinating new activity because there is no wrong answer in this question.

4

Purchases of Bees

For the novice beekeeper, purchasing bees is the easiest and least expensive way to start an apiary. Hive nuclei or kit bees are the two most widely used ways to obtain bees.

• Place Bee Purchase: To place an order for a shipment of bees, contact a local beekeeping association or supplier. A queen, multiple employees, and a feeder full with sugar syrup should be included in many transactions. You will receive instructions from the bee maker on how to transfer the bees kit to their new location and add workers to the queen bee. She flies safely within a customized cage in your bees pack.

Oh Using the lengthy form is the most typical way to present the Queen. As the new monarch eventually eats their way into the food gap in their cage, worker bees get to meet him.

• Hive Nucleus: A hive nucleus is even available for purchase. A half-sized colony is referred to as a nucleus, or simply "nuc". Five frame nuc scales are the most widely used. You receive five frames with pollen, eggs, brood (baby eggs), peas, and queen. You can get started with colony development by purchasing a nuc. The honeycomb will transfer pests and illnesses from the donor colony to your hive, making this tactic slightly riskier than using kit bees.

Speak with a local beekeeping association to find out where in your city is best to purchase safe bees.

Viewing Bees: Untamed, The term for these bee colonies that are occasionally spotted in the wild is swarms. Since they require additional area for their expanding colony, bees also divide their territory. Honey bee swarming is a normal action that occurs primarily in the spring. Since the bees seem to be well-mannered, it's not difficult to capture a swarm. Wearing clean clothes is still important, though. It could also be a good idea to have a cigarette and sugar-water syrup with you to appease the irritable bees.

You can collect bees on tree branches by taking out the office and placing the department inside a jar and giving it a little shake. Just like you would with a dustpan, you can gently rub bees with cardboard to send them into a pot on a level surface or fence post. Smoke puffed behind them can also be used to guide them, causing them to push in the opposite direction (into the container). Bees should be moved from the jar to a hive and gently turned against it.

On a branch, bees are swarming: Having a home, however, isn't necessarily more comfortable. There could be a sickness or inadequate genetic makeup in wild bees. The Queen is remains elusive among wild bees, having either been wounded or killed.

It doesn't follow that you have to put up with it just because you can see it. Since certain jurisdictions have laws defining what constitutes "land," stealing specific bees could be considered theft if the tree branch is in your neighbor's yard. Before attempting to trap wild bees, check the local codes.

Depending on the conditions in your area, choose the best method for obtaining bees. If your town has a beekeeping group, they can assist you in gathering a swarm of wild bees or provide information on where to purchase a starter colony.

Methods for Transporting Bees

There is something intrinsically scary about opening a beehive. It is true that the package contains thousands of "stinging insects" after all. The experience of opening a colony can be exciting, fascinating, and even comforting until you become used to managing them and realize that none of them will want to sting you (since they will die if they do). The bees are teaching you how to behave, so be calm, cautious, vigilant, and courteous. When you smell the honey and propolis, hear the calming hum of the bees, and see the hive's coordinated movements, all of the world's problems will seem to fade away. This requires your complete attention and devotion. All you'll receive is an odd sting if you take care not to kill bees (which is the main source of stinging), treat them gently, and utilize the equipment and safety clothing correctly.

Although a sting hurts, it is only a little annoyance and nothing to be alarmed of if you quickly scrape it off with your fingernail or a bee tool.

The main tool used to prevent stings is the cigarette. The guard bees are deterred and forced out of locations where you don't want them, such as the top bar where you have to position your fingertips to remove a tag, by a hint of smoke. A smoker that is well-lit can smoke for hours at a time if necessary.

On an empty smoker, begin. A good light at the bottom, loads of fuel above, and something akin to a cloth on top are necessary to partially extinguish a fire that is exploding upward. With the help of your hive gadget, light a medium-sized (8"–10" square) piece of newspaper with a flame or lighter, push it into the smoker, add more coal, and pump the bellows hard until a strong, hot spark appears. Add a small amount additional fuel and pump it out before it burns thoroughly. Next add more coal to the smoker and cover it with a piece of cloth that covers nearly all of the flames, allowing a small amount of air to pass through so that smoke and air can escape. Once the amount of dense, clear, cold smoke is reached, stop pumping the bellows. A small amount of smoke, not much, will emerge from the sput if the bellows are not pumped. You can use any natural fiber or cellulosic yarn as fuel, like burlap, corncobs, cotton rags, pine needles, wood chips or ashes, sawdust, or sticks. Anything potentially dangerous should be avoided, such as heat-treated wood, cedarwood, synthetic materials, baler twine, and compounds that release fumes. Upon finishing the session, cover the smoker hole with a cork, turn it upside down to stop the airflow, and extinguish the flames. In roughly ten minutes, it will be fantastic.

When you ignite a fire again, discard the charcoal and utilize it to start the fire off well. Never take out hot coals! It follows that numerous forest fires have been started.

Even if a smoker is more effective, you can still use a spray bottle filled with a thin sugar syrup (approximately one part sugar to two parts water) to assist relax the bees.

Even if they don't hurt, bees can still be unsettling, so always wear a veil to keep them away from your face. If a bee is about to fly out of the cover, stay motionless, move away from the hive, remove the lid, and turn it upside down.

Get a mask and gloves, but don't use them until you come across a soiled colony. If necessary at first, wear them; however, gradually wean off of them as Your confidence in managing the bees increases. Gloves protect your hands from Any bees that are beneath your fingers, crush them, and cause irritation to settlement. They'll make jokes about everyone in your vicinity, and they'll as soon as you take off your clothes.

When the weather is warm, around midday, open your hive. When a honey flow is in progress, we are exceptionally sweet. Session ends when a rainstorm is approaching or in the late afternoon, as they get more intense. Just be mindful of your neighbors and don't disturb the bees if they are nearby, enjoy a picnic or a dip in their pool. Living on the safe side, give them a container of honey every now and then.

Reach around the door to the hive and take a puff of smoke from the side or back. Take off the outer layer and smoke from below. In cases where it is severely imprisoned, gently press the corners upward with a block or stone to break the propolis adhesive. Take off the top cover and place it facedown on the table. Lift the hive tool and push it up beneath one inner lid corner. Pry the other edge as well if it's still trapped. You can also operate two devices—one in each hand—on the hive. Raise the inner cover of the gadget, hold it in your hand (palm style), smoke a little under it, and hold it up next to the hive, the bees, and everything else. Bees are placed in a position where they cannot be kicked, so take care not to kill any of them.

You can now begin drawing the initial frame. In a handy and safe spot, put your foot as close to the bee as you can. Choose a building to take from the hand that is closest to you, usually the second. Ideally, the Queen will receive the fewest frames because the outer frames are meant to be fastened to the burr comb box. The frame you've chosen will stand out if there is burr comb between the top plates and it breaks out from the surrounding frames. With your hive tool, loosen all of the frame's ends and pry it sideways. Making use of the nearby frame as a fulcrum, place the end of the device nearest to one end under the top bar and pry it upward. Pry the opposite side by catching the top bar adjacent to the edge. When the structure reaches the various frames, hold it firmly in both hands and raise it straight up gradually, giving any bees caught in between the frames a chance to escape. Turning or tilting the frame can kill your queen and sting you in addition to crushing bees.

Smoke the bees on top of the bottom box, force the clustered bees onto the plates, then puff some smoke beneath the super to bring it back on the hive.

Holding the super, tip it over such that only one corner touches the bottom of the smaller table. Give the bees an opportunity to clear out of the way by carefully wriggling one side into the dish. As you gently lower the box into its destination, shake it up and down a little. If done correctly, there should be no sound of smashed bees, and you can walk away without getting stung while removing the top and inner covers in the same manner.

Providing Meals For Emerging Bees

It may cross your mind to question if your bees have enough food to survive the winter, or if they would starve to death. Additionally, you might like to encourage your colony to prepare itself appropriately in the spring for maximum protection.

What time and method do you feed your bees then?

Are You Feeding Bees Correctly?

To avoid having to feed the honeybees, you would leave a plenty of honey in a perfect habitat for them. However, occasionally there is a poor nectar flow, which leaves the bees without adequate honey stored, especially if you have a new colony that was established this spring.

It can be abundant with bees when you can easily remove your hive. To keep from starving throughout the winter, the expanding colony needs at least 50–60 pounds of stored honey. If you find out early enough in the season, similar to fall, you can begin feeding them. You don't eat until winter and early spring, but you still need to feed the bees. Use fondant or granulated sugar if possible, especially on chilly winter days.

You may feed your bees with a variety of feeder models; just make sure the one you choose fits both their demands and the conditions in which they live. Certain feeding materials work better than others. A simple inverted bucket feeder with a few tiny holes drilled through the middle of the lid works great as a hive-top feeder. Mason jars can be inverted in this manner as well.

In the winter, wait until it's at least 40 degrees outside with little to no heat before opening the hive to inspect or feed the bees. Inspecting frames should never be done outside in temperatures below sixty degrees Fahrenheit.

One thing to consider is if you should encourage the growth of larvae when feeding bees. Granulated sugar, for instance, doesn't aid in the growth of brood because of its lower water content than other feed kinds. Don't feed it more than it desires. Overfeeding can result in an excessive number of brood or bee swarms.

Honey that has been kept can be fed back to your bees. The best food available to bees is baby. But never used to purchase honey, as it can bring pollution and illness to your colony! Occasionally, when feeding the bees in an emergency, beekeepers would set aside a black, strong-colored, or other "off" baby.

If not, create sugar syrup or subsist on sugar powder.

Recipes Using Sugar Syrup Pollen Patties In addition to providing them with pollen patties when necessary, bees require protein. Either create them yourself or get them as dry powder. Position the polen-filled patty atop the posts. If you are worried about your bees, utilize early spring pollen patties since dust is necessary for raising the brood in the early spring.

Fondant and Confectionery Sugars In winter, even in an emergency, fondant and sugar candies will be given if the sugar syrup is too cold.

To make sugar candy, combine 12 pounds of sugar with 1/4 cup of hot water and well stir. After 15 minutes of simmering, stir in 1 teaspoon of tartar cream and 1/2 teaspoon of salt. Allow it cool slightly before giving it a good stir and ladling into plates. Flip the platter over the frames holding the cluster after it has cooled down enough. Don't forget to test the hard candy recipe as well.

Pour a fourth of the water into a big pot and bring it to a boil. Turn off the oil and stir in five pounds of powdered sugar. Return the water to a boil and stir once the sugar has dissolved. Utilizing a cookie as a thermometer, bring a mixture to 260–270 degrees Fahrenheit, or a hard candy consistency. Pour onto cookie sheets coated with wax paper or into molds. After cooling down, divide into smaller pieces and place wax paper on them to keep them frozen.

Purchasing already-established colonies

Although it is not a good idea for novice beekeepers to buy established colonies, seasoned beekeepers might view this as a practical approach to expand their province count. Assessing the true market value, assuming illness risk, and dealing with material that is very variable in quality and probably not of standard measures are some of the issues that arise when purchasing secondhand equipment and bees.

Beginners are usually ill-equipped to manage a full-sized area, even if they can receive financial rewards from an established colony in the first season. Buying smaller units, such as packages or nucs, early in the beekeeping season can help a beginner develop more persuasive beekeeping techniques as well as an improvement in trust and management abilities as the colony grows larger.

5

Basics of Beehive Inspection

Monitoring your bees' progress requires daily observation of the hives. It's important to identify issues early on and find solutions. Examining the beehive is essential for both apiarists and beekeepers with a single colony. Every beehive has different maintenance and testing schedules. While certain hives may need to be inspected frequently, many hives may be viewed infrequently or never at all. In their first year, beehives typically require more frequent inspections. In its second year, the hive would require a lot less controls.

1. Points to be aware of There are a number of things you might look for when inspecting a beehive. Usually, the stability of the beehive's structure and the colony's well-being come first. You can establish the baselines for basic problem-sensing by routinely watching and listening to the bees. It can also be utilized by someone who has a keen sense of smell to see how things are doing in their beehives! Beekeepers need to be aware that it's necessary to periodically assess acceptable brood quality. In a colony, review provides an opportunity to evaluate the health of the brood. Bee population declines indicate a family's bad health. Should you discover a decrease in brood in your hive, you may want to use a brood booster or feed the bees pollen patties.

2. You can forecast colony production by inspecting beehives. Taking an opportunity to choose the room where your bees should reside. This guarantees that additional frames or hive boxes are added. Until it becomes

necessary, beekeepers will continue to create more bee space. Bee populations that are larger are more likely to withstand the challenging environment.

Important Information: When a bee colony outgrows its living quarters, it may divide or relocate.

Hive separation is one method among many for controlling bee colony sizes. When it's time to remove your bee colony, the beehive check will let you know.

One strategy for controlling swarms is colony division. Swarming setups, such as queen cups, should alert you during beehive inspections.

3. Items to avoid wearing During bee inspections, refrain from donning colognes, perfumes, or scented hair sprays. More often than not, bees are drawn to delicious smells when you're taking an exam. Recall to take off all jewelry, especially rings. Dealing with pain would be more natural for you if you were stung on your palm while in a circle. Rings aren't increasing, which explains why. Bees may find leather and wool textiles repulsive. The materials transmit a significant amount of noticeable body odor to flies, and their aroma aggravates bees.

4. Attire Because of their purpose and design, bees get you close to them during an inspection of a hive. Mostly, beekeepers need protection. If you are near a beehive or during beehive inspections, you must wear protective gear to ensure proper security. All it takes to get you kicked out of the hive and enrage a ton of worker bees is one irate bee. A smoker and a hive machine are essential tools for beehive inspections, in addition to the safety gear.

Safety suggestions During a beehive check, if a bee tries to go under your beekeeping gear or through your scarf, don't worry too much. Avoid squeezing the bees by moving away from the hive.

If you are at a safe distance, just remove the mask or veil from each beehive. You should take a healthy approach to solving the bee problem while wearing your beekeeping costume.

The bees can get worse by thrashing and exhibiting other anxious behaviors. You run the greater risk of making a mistake when you wait.

5. The Amount of Time to Check a Beehive Does each opening last a different amount of time? In accordance with their availability to do such

an investigation, beekeepers may also alter their plans for inspecting their hives. Beekeepers should not disturb the bees, even if they must keep an eye on their hives and colonies. A typical hive needs to be inspected every two to three weeks. Every seven to ten days, a more recent swarm needs to be inspected for progress tracking.

Beekeepers gradually increase the intervals between hive inspections since a beehive that is occupied by live bees lasts longer. Be aware that it takes a day for the bees to recuperate from any disturbance to their colony. Thus, it would have been preferable to employ that time instead of wasting it gathering nectar and pollen for the hive.

This is limited to recently mounted bee colonies. Should you take too much from them, they might wish to move out of the beehive and find another place to remain.

Beekeepers who are new to the hobby can worry about the health of their hive. Their inexperience may cause them to open their beehives far too frequently.

The colony will become stressed when hives are inspected very frequently. Swarms invading and surrounding beehives are unfamiliar to them. Beekeeping is not appropriate when colony conflicts occur.

The queen will be killed or the bees will abandon the colony. Low-frequency shifts to the queens were observed in others. Examining a hive is a good idea, but don't go overboard. Make sure you have a solid justification for every beehive inspection you do.

6. If not starting a hive, this is also a challenging period for bees to establish a colony. Bees require recovery time following any interventions made during hive inspections. To prevent your bees' wellbeing and productivity from declining, you shouldn't open your hive too frequently. The aptitude for inspecting beehives is also evaluated by the environment. Beekeepers are urged to cease opening beehives during cold weather. Weather that is moderate is ideal for beehive inspections. It isn't expected to be chilly, windy, or dry. Rain or the threat of rain is also inappropriate. It is extremely bad for your bee colony to have brood frames raised. Reduced growth occurs when brood is affected by the cold.

In order to survive the winter, bees use honey as fuel to light the hive. Opening a beehive in the winter increases pressure to keep the hive dry.

Since bees can consume more pollen, the colony's requirement for resources during the winter months is reduced.

7. The Optimal Time of Day to Examine the Beehive Make sure the body does not hide or impede the beehive entrances so that bees can inspect the hive at a pleasant and convenient moment for them. Expert beekeepers know when to schedule a beehive check. They can forecast the time of day when the majority of bees are out searching for food and inspecting the hive. It explains why there are less frustrated bees in the nest. Between 11 AM and 2 PM, you have the ideal window of opportunity to complete the checks. You need to watch out for Queen Bee closely during the inspections.

Regarding the Queen You don't have to see the Queen to inspect a beehive.

A successful queen bee in the beehive is indicated by eggs laid in cells. If a beekeeper is unfamiliar with identifying the queen, they might brand her for easier identification.

Depending on daylight Beekeepers should avoid carrying lighting equipment when doing beehive inspections as it poses health risks. When the beehive is opened and put back together, beekeepers rely on natural lighting. The sun is higher in the atmosphere between 11 AM and 2 PM, which gives those times of day an extra advantage. This lets you see inside the beehive when you open it up to inspect it. You will have less light to work with if you do a beehive check within these authorized hours.

8. Inspecting: During wintering, bee activity is reduced. They miss the top and disperse far throughout the hive. We'll get through checking the winter beehive quickly. It is preferable for us when the temperature is not too low. You could only get a quick glance. It's ideal to feed your bees during your winter beehive inspection. Beekeepers feed sugar cakes and protein patties to their hives throughout the winter. Avoid tearing out the entire beehive in the winter. Only the top cover and the inner cover can be removed by beekeepers doing a beehive check in the winter. You can take off the top sheet of any insulation that covers your colony. For more information, see our piece on practical beekeeping advice for the winter.

Making Use of a Checklist for Beehive Inspection

Examining Beehives

Beekeepers might utilize a checklist on a beehive while doing beehive inspections. You can complete all of the scheduled beehive inspection tasks precisely if you have a list. It enables you to record your actions during an inspection, and together, let's make a history of the health of your hives.

Beekeepers may use a uniform checklist for several types of checks. You can add additional space and set a number of items on a checklist. Due to their peculiarities, beehives may require their own checklist. Watch out for different technical concerns with different designs of beehives. Bees may draw improperly from the comb in some beehive designs. This burr-comb needs to be picked up right away during beehive inspections. With the help of the tutorial, you can spot themes and patterns rapidly.

There are countless areas and facets of beehive integrity that you should include in your inspection checklist, such as (but not restricted to): overall look of the hive Signs of illnesses and pests Weather and procreation are dominant.

I think getting a nuc locally from other beekeepers is the greatest method for a newbie to acquire bees. You will meet a fellow beekeeper who may be able to assist you in times of need, and your bees won't have to be exported, which is typically stressful.

Doubt over the location of the hives

A field full of beehives

One of the most frequent problems a new beekeeper faces is deciding where to install their hive. You possess specialized expertise if you have been involved in the activity for a long time. The economics, chemical products, and climate change all have a significant influence on human behavior in the modern era.

Most beginning beekeepers begin in their backyard. If you live outside of a city, this is an easy method to get started. However, there are difficulties if you live next to a road or among other neighbors. Because bees travel great distances to obtain nectar, several books and websites claim you may put your hive nearly anyplace.

I occasionally ponder whether this person has ever been close to a beehive. It is a challenge because, yes, bees fly great distances to obtain their nectar. No apiary should be situated in a way that could endanger animals, humans, or bees in general.

You must locate a location with top-notch floral supply. In addition, it should have the proper quantity of sun, a nearby water source with drainage, and protection from predators and vandals for your bees.

Bees require a floral supply.

It is a common misconception that bees will prefer a flower-filled field. However, may I ask you this: are you happy with every food that the supermarket sells?

I'd venture to say not. Similar to other bees, not every bloom in your backyard yields nectar to be collected.

Only a small portion of the world's estimated 20,000 species of bees are honeybees. In order to pollinate plant species in their native habitat, various types of honey bees have evolved. In Italy, for instance, citrus blooms are what draw bees. An insect would disregard a citrus flower if it was absent from its usual environment. It is impossible for the Africanized bees that pollinate the Amazon in Brazil to be transported to the south of the country to fertilize eucalyptus trees. It will be beneficial to you in your beekeeping endeavors to be aware of the local plant species and native types.

Working with queen bees

Without it, Queen, a beehive cannot exist. And a lot of novice beekeepers fail to recognize when their colony is queenless, mainly because they assume that the behavior of the colony will drastically change. A beehive without a queen will not immediately exhibit a difference in behavior from the colony.

Because the workers will be spending all of their time foraging instead of caring for the larvae, there will be a plenty of honey and healthy traffic at the beehive entrance. It will be too late for the colony to survive if the beekeeper fails to notice the decline in population and if the colony has gone too long without a queen.

Every day, a queen can lay close to 2000 eggs. Indicative of possible queenlessness in your beehive is the absence of brood throughout the warm season. Another possibility is that you'll realize the queen needs to be changed. The elderly queen might be stumbling and not laying as many eggs as she once did. The colony's behavior is not what it ought to be. Or the province produces little. You should adjust your queen as a result of all these indicators.

The good news is that a queen may be changed in a variety of ways, and bees will usually accept a new queen quite a high percentage of the time. The bees also take care of a lot of the work for you; they know when a new queen is needed. They also take action. To learn more about the process, see my post "How many queen bees are in a beehive?"

Make sure the old queen is gone or dead a day before introducing the new queen you ordered if you are going to introduce the new queen. The employees will begin producing eggs and eventually turn into drones if you wait too long to introduce a new queen.

Market demand and honey prices

When the expense of beekeeping exceeds the cost of the product, beekeepers are more likely to give up on the hobby if they are doing it for financial gain. We have previously discussed the various difficulties that beekeeping suffers today, but the primary cause of beekeepers' resignations is their expulsion from the market. For instance, in Uruguay, one of the world's most established suppliers of honey, 30% of beekeepers gave up last year. You won't have this issue if you decide to take up beekeeping as a pastime. However, you will eventually have more honey than you can eat, at which point you may choose to sell some. Indeed, beekeeping is regarded as an extremely sustainable means of rescuing individuals from poverty, and numerous governments across the globe endorse it.

As with anything, the price of honey varies greatly depending on supply and demand. Additionally, you may profit from or suffer the effects of a drought or flood on the other side of the globe if you are in a large honey-consuming market. Once you started to generate more honey, I would advise doing research and developing a plan for selling the product. Start by selling to your friends, then consider distributing your goods through neighborhood companies. Baby for sale might be a lucrative venture.

Low nectar

A lack of nectar-producing flowers is known as a nectar dearth. It also usually occurs in the winter. However, identifying and controlling a nectar shortage—particularly during the summer—can be difficult for a novice beekeeper. Summertime nectar shortage is brought either by high temperatures and drought, or little precipitation.

In addition to fewer nectar-producing flowers, another possible outcome of a nectar dearth is a robust colony trying to rob a weaker colony of its nectar reserve. When a colony loses its food source, beefighting and death spirals out of control, allowing other predators—like hornets—to attack and decimate the colony.

The spread of parasites from the weak colony to the stronger one, such as the varroa mite, is another effect. One of the reasons a healthy colony could fail in a few weeks is because of this. The apiculturists are left wondering what went wrong.

Once you've identified a nectar dearth (read this article to learn what a nectar dearth is and how to survive one), you can safeguard your bees by doing the following actions:

Feed them syrup. To keep other colonies from attracting attention, do not place a feeder within the hive's entrance. To maintain food inside the beehive, use an internal feeder.

If you plan to feed them, stay away from essential oils and other items made specifically for nectar deficiency. Bees from great distances will be drawn to them. Once the nectar is inside, don't worry—the bees will find the meal.

Close the higher gates to minimize entry into the colony. One of your first actions to defend the area from intruders should be feeding the animals, whether you want to do so or not.

Keep moist frames and communal feeders away from your apiary since this invites stronger colonies to congregate close to your weaker colony.

After you begin, challenges will become easier.

I am aware that beekeeping, particularly for novice beekeepers, may appear like a difficult endeavor. That being said, once you start reading up on beekeeping, learning about it, and gaining some practical experience, all of these difficulties and issues will seem to go away.

The variety of beekeeping makes it an excellent activity because you may learn new things about it all the time. I hope you will find it as appealing as I do.

Activities in Colonies: Seasonal Cycles

A hive of honey bees consists of a few hundred to several thousand drones (males who are sexually exploited), a queen (a female who has reached sexual maturity), and several thousand workers (females who are sexually immature). The number of drones varies based on the season and size of the colony. Usually, there is only one queen each colony, and her only job is to lay eggs. The honey (a food source of carbohydrates) and pollen (a food source of proteins) that the bees store in their loosely arranged clusters atop several wax combs are also used by the young bees to rear older adults. Seasons influence a colony's activity. A honey bee colony may observe the months of September through December as the start of a new year. The settlement's state during this time of year has a significant impact on how prosperous it is the following year. 1Entomologist for research, Science and Education Administration, Carl Hayden Center for Bee Research, Tuscon, AZ 85719.

A decrease in the quantity of nectar and pollen entering the hive in the fall results in less brood rearing and a declining population. The percentage of old bees in the colony declines with the age of the queen and her ability to lay eggs. The older bees slowly wither away during the winter, while the younger ones survive. To prevent cold air from entering the hive, propolis that is extracted from tree buds is used to seal all of the opening's crevices. The workers pull the drones from the hive and prevent them from returning when the amount of nectar in the field becomes scarce, starving them to death.

The consumption of winter honey stocks decreases with the removal of hums. The bees start to cluster tightly as the temperature falls to 57° F. The brood—which consists of eggs, larvae, and pupae—is kept warm in this cluster by the heat produced by the bees, which is approximately 93° F. The queen bee's egg-laying diminishes and may cease completely around October or November, regardless of whether pollen is kept in the combs. The colony faces its worst endurance test during the chilly winters. Egg-laying and brood-rearing typically never cease in subtropical, tropical, and warm winter climates.

The bees cluster closer together to conserve heat when the temperature drops. The bees inside the cluster are kept warm by the tightly packed outer layer of bees. The group grows and shrinks with variations in temperature.

Within the cluster, the bees have access to the food storage. The cluster moves to cover new sections of the comb that hold honey during warm seasons. The bees may choke to death within inches from the infant if a very extended cold spell prevents cluster migration.

The queen remains inside the cluster and follows it around as it changes positions. Rich colonies that receive plenty of honey and pollen in the fall will start to stimulate the queen, who will lay eggs in late December or early January—even in the northern parts of the United States. This fresh brood helps replenish the bees that have perished over the winter. Pollen reserves accumulated during the previous fall govern the degree of early brood raising. Colonies that do not have enough pollen postpone brood rearing until they gather fresh powder from spring flowers, and these colonies often have fewer individuals when they come out of winter. Nevertheless, regions with an abundance of young bees generated during the fall and an ample supply of pollen and honey for winter usually have a robust population in the spring. The colony population typically falls throughout the winter because elderly bees continue to die.

Springtime Exercise

The longer days and fresh nectar and pollen supplies in the early spring encourage brood rearing. In order to prepare food for their brood, the bees additionally gather water to control temperature and dissolve granular or viscous honey. This time of year, drones will be nonexistent or hard to find. Later in the spring, the colony's population grows quickly, and the percentage of young bees rises. The number of field workers rises in tandem with population growth. Honey and pollen surpluses may build up as a result of field bees gathering nectar and pollen in greater quantities than are required to support brood raising.

The cluster grows larger and drone production increases as the days get longer and the temperature rises. The nest space of the colony is crowded as a result of an increase in adult bees and brood rearing. At the nest's entrance, more bees are seen. Seeing the bees creep out and hang in a swarm around the door on a warm afternoon is a dead giveaway that the area is overcrowded.

In addition, the queen boosts drone egglaying in anticipation of the colony's natural swarming division. These factors are combined with congested living conditions. The bees breed a new queen in addition to caring for workers and drones. The development of a few larvae that would typically become worker bees is accelerated by feeding them royal jelly, an extraordinary gland meal, and reconstructing their cells to fit the larger queen. Individual colonies as well as bee races and strains have different production rates for queen cells.

The colony will attempt to grow by creating new combs if food and space are available, notwithstanding how congested it is. The older combs are utilized for growing brood and storing pollen, whereas the newer combs are often used for honey storage.

Overflowing

The colony will swarm during the warmer hours of the day when the first virgin queen is about ready to emerge and before the main nectar flow. About half of the bees and the elderly queen will hurry out the door together.

Following a few minutes of aerial flight, they will congregate atop a tree limb or other like object. Depending on how long it takes the scouting bees to locate a new home, this cluster often lasts for an hour or two. The cluster disperses and flies to a place after one has been identified. As soon as they get to the original location, they swiftly build combs, begin raising their young, and gather pollen and nectar. Although it can happen at any time from April to October, swarming often takes place in the Central, Southern, and Western States between March and June.

Nectar, pollen, propolis, and water are collected by the surviving bees in the parent colony when the swarm leaves. In addition, they protect the entrance, tend to the eggs, larvae, and nourishment, and construct combs. New drones are raised to produce a male population that will mate with the virgin queen. She eats honey, grooms herself for a little while, and then leaves her cage to search the colony for other queens that are in competition with her. All but one of the queens are destroyed in mortal combat. Upon reaching around one week of age, the survivor travels to the skies to mate with one or more drones. Upon mating, the drones perish, but the mated queen becomes the new queen mother and returns to the nest. She was neglected before mating, but now nurse bees take care of her. The mated queen starts laying eggs in three or four days.

The colony temperature needs to be maintained at roughly 93° F throughout the sweltering summer months. In order to accomplish this, the bees gather water and disseminate it inside the nest, where air movement causes it to evaporate inside the cluster.

At its busiest in early summer, the colony focuses on gathering nectar and pollen, storing honey for the winter ahead, and reaching its peak number. Everything a colony does after reproduction is focused on surviving the winter. The summer is a good time to store extra food supplies. The longest daytime hours allow for the greatest amount of foraging; yet, precipitation or a drought may decrease the amount of nectar and pollen that blooms provide. The summer months are when winter supplies are gathered. The beekeeper can withdraw some honey and yet have enough for the colony to survive if there is enough honey stored.

Beeswax and Honey Harvesting

The cappings that you cut off during the honey extraction process indicate your annual significant wax harvest.For every 100 pounds of honey you collect, you should expect to receive one or two pounds of wax. A honey press combined with a Top Bar hive will yield an even larger beeswax bonanza.

There are numerous applications for this cleaned and melted wax. It will cost you more money per pound to retrieve this prize because wax is more valuable than honey. These are some recommendations:

Let gravity extract as much honey as it can from the wax. Allow the wax to drain for several days. This procedure is made much simpler by using a twin uncapping tank. Pour warm (not hot) water into a five-gallon plastic pail containing the drained wax. To remove any last bits of honey, use a paddle or your hands to slosh the wax in the water. Repeat this washing procedure until the water runs clear after draining the wax through a colander or a honey strainer. To melt the cleaned wax, put it in a double boiler.

Since beeswax is extremely flammable, it should always be melted in a double boiler. Never melt beeswax over an open flame. Furthermore, do not, under any circumstances, even for a split second, remove the melting wax. Please shut off the burner if you need to use the restroom.

Remove any residue from the melted beeswax by straining it through two layers of cheesecloth.

To ensure that the wax is free of all contaminants, remelt and re-strain as needed.

To store the rendered wax for later use, it can be poured into a block mold.

One possible use is an old cardboard milk carton. You may easily remove the melted wax from the container by peeling off the carton, leaving behind a substantial block of pure, light-golden beeswax.

In conclusion

Beekeeping, also known as apiculture, is a popular hobby among people for a variety of purposes, including producing honey and other bee products like wax and propolis, or helping with agricultural cross-pollination, breeding, and sales. Before beginning, everyone interested in beekeeping should always take care of the local legal requirements related to the activity. Additionally, beehives need to be situated close to flowers, a water source, and areas with adequate sunlight. The best site will be one that is difficult for bee predators to reach.

Since bees are essential to pollinate plants, which in turn helps plants produce oxygen—which is necessary for human survival—and because bee populations around the world have declined recently, now is the ideal time to start a beekeeping business, even if it's just as a hobby.